At Issue

The H1N1 Flu

DEC 2010

Other Books in the At Issue Series:

At Issue

The H1N1 Flu

Noah Berlatsky, Book Editor

GREENHAVEN PRESS
A part of Gale, Cengage Learning

Detroit • New York • San Francisco • New Haven, Conn • Waterville, Maine • London

Christine Nasso, *Publisher*
Elizabeth Des Chenes, *Managing Editor*

© 2011 Greenhaven Press, a part of Gale, Cengage Learning.

Gale and Greenhaven Press are registered trademarks used herein under license.

For more information, contact:
Greenhaven Press
27500 Drake Rd.
Farmington Hills, MI 48331-3535
Or you can visit our Internet site at gale.cengage.com

For product information and technology assistance, contact us at

Gale Customer Support, 1-800-877-4253
For permission to use material from this text or product, submit all requests online at
www.cengage.com/permissions

Further permissions questions can be e-mailed to permissionrequest@cengage.com

Articles in Greenhaven Press anthologies are often edited for length to meet page requirements. In addition, original titles of these works are changed to clearly present the main thesis and to explicitly indicate the author's opinion. Every effort is made to ensure that Greenhaven Press accurately reflects the original intent of the authors. Every effort has been made to trace the owners of copyrighted material.

Cover image © Images.com/Corbis.

LIBRARY OF CONGRESS CATALOGING-IN-PUBLICATION DATA

The H1N1 flu / Noah Berlatsky, book editor.
    p. cm. -- (At issue)
    Includes bibliographical references and index.
    ISBN 978-0-7377-5089-8 (hardcover) -- ISBN 978-0-7377-5090-4 (pbk.)
    1. H1N1 influenza. I. Berlatsky, Noah.
    RA644.I6H26 2010
    614.5'18--dc22

                                                                2010010291

Printed in the United States of America
1 2 3 4 5 6 7 14 13 12 11 10

Contents

Introduction

H1N1 Virus

No one is certain how the H1N1 virus, also known as swine flu, got its start. The first identified case occurred in La Gloria, Mexico, in the state of Veracruz. In Feburary, 2009, the town experienced a wave of flu so serious that state health workers were dispatched. Of the 3,000 townspeople, "1,300 sought . . . medical help" and "450 were diagnosed with acute respiratory infections," according to Olga R. Rodriguez, writing in an April 28, 2009 article in *The Huffington Post*.

One of the residents who became sick was a five-year-old boy named Edgar Hernandez. Hernandez came down with flulike symptoms in late March. Samples of his mucus revealed that he had the first confirmed case of what became known as swine flu.

How Hernandez contracted the flu is unclear. La Gloria is home to numerous pig-breeding farms. Although his own family did not work with pigs, it is possible that someone "who worked with pigs became infected and passed it on to other people," according to Joshua Partlow, writing in an April 29, 2009 *Washington Post* article. Transmission of flu viruses from pigs to humans is not common but does occur. According to *The Sydney Morning Herald* in an April 27, 2009 article, "there were 12 known transmissions of swine flu to humans" in the United States between 2005 and February 2009.

Whether Hernandez got the virus directly from pigs, he probably was not the first human affected. Even before the virus moved to humans, however, it seems likely that it had been "evolving for a long time," according to Laurie Garrett in a May 3, 2009 *Newsweek* article. Garrett noted that the virus was "a mosaic of swine/bird/human flu," and added that it probably had been "aided in its transformation by the ecology of industrial-scale pig farming in North America."

The virus was soon discovered in other parts of Mexico. The first death occurred on April 12, when a 39-year-old woman succumbed to the disease in central Mexico. By April 24, there were "more than 900 suspected cases and 62 deaths linked to swine flu" in Mexico, according to David Batty and Abigail Edge writing in an April 29, 2009 article in *The Guardian*. The majority of cases and deaths were in Mexico City. By April 26, 81 deaths had been linked to the virus, and there were 20 cases of the virus reported in New York City. By April 29, the number of those suspected to have been killed by swine flu had risen to 159, and cases had been reported in Europe, South Korea, Malaysia, New Zealand, and Australia.

By April 25, Mexico City residents were wearing surgical masks outdoors, and health officials were inspecting airports to try to detect infected passengers. Mexican President Felipe Calderón declared "emergency powers . . . including isolating those who . . . contracted the virus, inspecting the homes of affected people and ordering the cancellation of public events," according to Marc Lacey and Elisabeth Malkin writing in *The New York Times* on April 25, 2009. Five days later, on April 30, Mexico suspended economic and governmental activity. The closure included "Schools, businesses and nonsessential offices," according to a May 1, 2009 article on the *Stratfor* Web site. This was a severe economic blow to the country, which was already reeling from the loss of tourism. Hotels in the tourist destination of Cancun reported "20% occupancy rates," according to journalist Suzanne Barbezat, and "Many airlines cancel[ed] flights to Mexico for lack of passengers."

Mexico's response to the swine flu outbreak was praised by the World Health Organization (WHO) representative, Philippe Lamy, who said the Mexican government had acted with "'responsibility and transparency,'" on May 6, 2009. On that date, schools and businesses reopened, and the worst of the infection in Mexico appeared to have passed. "[E]xperts said the new H1N1 virus might be no more severe than normal flu," according to a Reuters report on May 4, 2009.

Nonetheless, H1N1 had not disappeared. On the contrary, the virus continued to spread, and in June 2009, WHO declared H1N1 a pandemic. Declaring H1N1 a pandemic did not necessarily mean that the flu virus was especially severe, or that it was likely to kill many people. What it did indicate was that the virus was "circulating in communities in widespread parts of the globe, and that all nations can eventually expect to see cases," according to Daniel J. DeNoon writing in a June 11, 2009 article on *WebMD*.

H1N1, then, was not as virulent as first feared, but it remained a worldwide threat. The viewpoints that follow discuss how dangerous the H1N1 virus might be, and how individuals and governments should respond to it.

1

H1N1 Meets the Criteria for an Influenza Pandemic

Margaret Chan

Margaret Chan is the director-general of the World Health Organization (WHO). She began her administrative career at WHO in 2003, and before that served as director of health for Hong Kong, where she managed outbreaks of avian influenza and of severe acute respiratory syndrome (SARS).

A new strain of the common H1N1 influenza virus has been detected. It has spread widely and quickly enough to be termed a pandemic. Luckily, the virus is of only moderate severity, and most patients recover. However, the situation will be closely monitored for any changes. Vaccines are being developed. Young people and pregnant women are hit especially hard by the virus, and these groups should take extra precautions.

In late April [2009], WHO announced the emergence of a novel influenza A virus [that is, a new type of a common strain of influenza].

This particular H1N1 strain has not circulated previously in humans. The virus is entirely new.

The virus is contagious, spreading easily from one person to another, and from one country to another. As of today [June 11, 2009], nearly 30,000 confirmed cases have been reported in 74 countries.

This is only part of the picture. With few exceptions, countries with large numbers of cases are those with good surveillance and testing procedures in place.

Margaret Chan, "World Now at the Start of 2009 Influenza Pandemic," World Health Organization Web site, June 11, 2009. Reproduced by permission.

Spread in several countries can no longer be traced to clearly-defined chains of human-to-human transmission. Further spread is considered inevitable.

Pandemic Criteria Have Been Met

I have conferred with leading influenza experts, virologists, and public health officials. In line with procedures set out in the International Health Regulations, I have sought guidance and advice from an Emergency Committee established for this purpose.

On the basis of available evidence, and these expert assessments of the evidence, the scientific criteria for an influenza pandemic have been met.

I have therefore decided to raise the level of influenza pandemic alert from phase 5 to phase 6.

The world is now at the start of the 2009 influenza pandemic.

We are in the earliest days of the pandemic. The virus is spreading under a close and careful watch.

No previous pandemic has been detected so early or watched so closely, in real-time, right at the very beginning. The world can now reap the benefits of investments, over the last five years, in pandemic preparedness.

The virus writes the rules, and this one, like all influenza viruses, can change the rules, without rhyme or reason, at any time.

We have a head start. This places us in a strong position. But it also creates a demand for advice and reassurance in the midst of limited data and considerable scientific uncertainty.

Thanks to close monitoring, thorough investigations, and frank reporting from countries, we have some early snapshots depicting spread of the virus and the range of illness it can cause.

We know, too, that this early, patchy picture can change very quickly. The virus writes the rules and this one, like all influenza viruses, can change the rules, without rhyme or reason, at any time.

Moderate Severity

Globally, we have good reason to believe that this pandemic, at least in its early days, will be of moderate severity. As we know from experience, severity can vary, depending on many factors, from one country to another.

On present evidence, the overwhelming majority of patients experience mild symptoms and make a rapid and full recovery, often in the absence of any form of medical treatment.

Worldwide, the number of deaths is small. Each and every one of these deaths is tragic, and we have to brace ourselves to see more. However, we do not expect to see a sudden and dramatic jump in the number of severe or fatal infections.

We know that the novel H1N1 virus preferentially infects younger people. In nearly all areas with large and sustained outbreaks, the majority of cases have occurred in people under the age of 25 years.

In some of these countries, around 2% of cases have developed severe illness, often with very rapid progression to life-threatening pneumonia.

Most cases of severe and fatal infections have been in adults between the ages of 30 and 50 years.

This pattern is significantly different from that seen during epidemics of seasonal influenza, when most deaths occur in frail elderly people.

Many, though not all, severe cases have occurred in people with underlying chronic conditions. Based on limited, preliminary data, conditions most frequently seen include respiratory diseases, notably asthma, cardiovascular disease, diabetes, autoimmune disorders, and obesity.

At the same time, it is important to note that around one third to half of the severe and fatal infections are occurring in previously healthy young and middle-aged people.

Without question, pregnant women are at increased risk of complications. This heightened risk takes on added importance for a virus, like this one, that preferentially infects younger age groups.

Finally, and perhaps of greatest concern, we do not know how this virus will behave under conditions typically found in the developing world. To date, the vast majority of cases have been detected and investigated in comparatively well-off countries.

A characteristic feature of pandemics is their rapid spread to all parts of the world.

Let me underscore two of many reasons for this concern. First, more than 99% of maternal deaths, which are a marker of poor quality care during pregnancy and childbirth, occurs in the developing world.

Second, around 85% of the burden of chronic diseases is concentrated in low- and middle-income countries.

Although the pandemic appears to have moderate severity in comparatively well-off countries, it is prudent to anticipate a bleaker picture as the virus spreads to areas with limited resources, poor health care, and a high prevalence of underlying medical problems. . . .

Remain Vigilant

A characteristic feature of pandemics is their rapid spread to all parts of the world. In the previous century, this spread has typically taken around 6 to 9 months, even during times when most international travel was by ship or rail.

Countries should prepare to see cases, or the further spread of cases, in the near future. Countries where outbreaks appear to have peaked should prepare for a second wave of infection.

Guidance on specific protective and precautionary measures has been sent to ministries of health in all countries. Countries with no or only a few cases should remain vigilant.

Countries with widespread transmission should focus on the appropriate management of patients. The testing and investigation of patients should be limited, as such measures are resource intensive and can very quickly strain capacities.

WHO has been in close dialogue with influenza vaccine manufacturers. I understand that production of vaccines for seasonal influenza will be completed soon, and that full capacity will be available to ensure the largest possible supply of pandemic vaccine in the months to come.

Pending the availability of vaccines, several non-pharmaceutical interventions can confer some protection.

WHO continues to recommend no restrictions on travel and no border closures.

Influenza pandemics, whether moderate or severe, are remarkable events because of the almost universal susceptibility of the world's population to infection.

We are all in this together, and we will all get through this, together.

2

The WHO Pandemic Alert for H1N1 Was a Sign of Corruption

Alex Newman

Alex Newman is a reporter and writer for the New American.

The Council of Europe is investigating the World Health Organization to determine whether drug companies influenced the decision to declare the H1N1 virus a pandemic. The H1N1 flu resulted in much less loss of life than predicted and was a waste of taxpayer money. The push to use untested vaccines may also have been dangerous. The episode shows that governments are not trustworthy and that the public needs to be more skeptical.

The Council of Europe [an organization of European states] is set to investigate the World Health Organization's swine flu campaign this month [January 2010] over allegations of improper influence from pharmaceutical companies in declaring the H1N1 "pandemic" [in June 2009] and the promotion of "inefficient" and potentially dangerous vaccination strategies.

Drug Companies Influenced Scientists

The resolution to launch the emergency inquiry was approved by the Parliamentary Assembly of the Council of Europe (PACE) and passed through the health committee unanimously. It states in part that "in order to promote their patented drugs and vaccines against flu, pharmaceutical companies influenced scientists and official agencies responsible for public health standards to alarm governments worldwide and make them squander tight health resources for inefficient vaccine strategies, and needlessly expose millions of healthy people to the risk of an unknown amount of side-effects of insufficiently tested vaccines."

[Dr. Wolfgang] Wodarg called the "false pandemic" one of the greatest medical scandals of the last [decade] and said that pharmaceutical companies influenced the whole process and needed to be held accountable.

"The 'bird-flu'-campaign (2005/06) [and] the 'swine-flu'-campaign[1] seem to have caused a great deal of damage not only to some vaccinated patients and to public health-budgets, but to the credibility and accountability of important international health-agencies," noted the resolution. "The Council of Europe and its member-states should ask for immediate investigations and consequences on their national levels as well as on the international level. The definition of an alarming pandemic must not be under the influence of drug-sellers."

Leading the charge for the probe is German epidemiologist Dr. Wolfgang Wodarg, the chairman of the PACE health committee and a medical doctor specializing in lung disease. "The victims among millions of needlessly vaccinated people must be protected by their states, and independent scientific clarification should provide evidence and transparency for national and—if necessary—European courts," Wodarg said in a statement.

Wodarg called the "false pandemic" one of the greatest medical scandals of the last century and said that pharmaceu-

1. Bird flu, a strain of H1N1 influenza virus, is seen as a possible major pandemic threat, especially if it mutates to transmit from person to person rather than just from bird to person. Swine flu is another name for the 2004 H1N1 virus.

tical companies influenced the whole process and needed to be held accountable. They were willing to "inflict bodily harm in their pursuit of profits," he said. Articles in the European press, starting in Denmark and spreading, have repeatedly called into question the myriad ties between vaccine manufacturers and decision makers in the United Nations' global health body.

Earlier this year the WHO redefined the term pandemic, lowering the threshold for an emergency declaration by removing the requirement of an "enormous" number of deaths. The WHO estimated that by the end of 2009, around 10,000 people had died from swine flu-linked complications. Seasonal influenza kills between 250,000 and 500,000 per year on average, according to the organization.

Deadly Pandemic Never Materialized

News reports earlier this year, citing the UN, warned of millions of deaths around the world unless nations promptly proceeded with the controversial vaccination schemes being promoted by the WHO—along with forking over billions of dollars. Since then, the disease has proved relatively mild despite the wild fearmongering campaigns waged by governments, such as the President's Council of Advisors on Science and Technology[, which] warned that 90,000 Americans could die from the H1N1 virus.

National governments should be ashamed of themselves for squandering billions of taxpayer dollars on . . . a virus that, so far, has been extremely mild compared [even to] the seasonal influenza.

The incident has reminded people of the avian flu scare. In September of 2005, the chief of the UN's bird flu preparations estimated that the epidemic could cause up to 150 million human deaths. So far, the WHO has confirmed slightly more than 250. The bird flu propaganda campaign will also be investigated by the "urgent" inquiry.

National governments should be ashamed of themselves for squandering billions of taxpayer dollars on an untested, unpopular vaccine for a virus that, so far, has been extremely mild compared [even to] the seasonal influenza. Governments are currently trying to get rid of the vaccine supplies. Global health authorities must be held accountable, though it's unfortunate that the charge is being led by a European supranational body instead of national legislatures.

The United States should get involved as well—starting with a complete withdrawal from the UN and its subsidiary bodies. [U.S. President Barack] Obama's declaration of a national emergency over swine flu is looking increasingly preposterous. Of course, Congress should also be held accountable for allowing this all to happen in America in the first place, despite the lack of constitutional authority to purchase or promote vaccines. But on the bright side of this whole scandal, citizens may start realizing that government is not a reliable resource for honest and accurate information.

3

China Overreacted to H1N1

Jonathan M. Metzl

Jonathan M. Metzl is a professor of psychiatry and women's studies and directs the Program in Culture, Health, and Medicine at the University of Michigan.

In order to defend against H1N1, China placed foreign travelers in uncomfortable and isolated quarantine conditions, even when there was little danger of infection. This violates international standards—it is a waste of money and needlessly endangers the health and well-being of the quarantined. A more measured response, unmotivated by xenophobia, fear, and prejudice, would be safer for both China and its visitors.

When I arrived in China late last month [June 2009], the hazmat-suited public officials who met my plane had the same question for each passenger: "Have you had contact with pigs?"[1] The officials took our temperatures, and then we were free to pass through customs and go on our way.

As a physician who had come to Shanghai to lecture at a Chinese medical school, I found it interesting to witness first-hand China's public health response to the H1N1 virus. The process seemed like overkill, and it had debatable public health benefits, but it didn't inconvenience me terribly. Or so I thought at the time.

Quarantined

The next evening, I returned from dinner to find two white-coated public health workers waiting for me in the lobby of

1. The H1N1 virus is thought to have originated in pigs.

Jonathan M. Metzl, "China's Ill-Considered Response to the H1N1 Virus," *L.A. Times*, July 12, 2009. Reproduced by permission of the author.

my hotel. Apparently, a passenger three rows in front and five seats across from me on the flight had tested positive for H1N1. I was given 30 minutes to pack my belongings. When I returned with my bags, I noticed that the hotel staff stood in the corner of the suddenly cleared lobby wearing surgical masks. "I have no symptoms whatsoever," I tried to explain, but the siren of the ambulance that sped to the front of the hotel drowned out my protestations. The back door opened to reveal three fellow American passengers from my flight. I climbed in, and we drove two hours in darkness.

The Chinese media have reported that travelers placed in quarantine are being held at five-star hotels, but if this is true, then the star system is in need of revision.

At 3 A.M., we arrived at a rural motel complex. Each of us was assigned to a single room and handed a letter. "Ladies and Gentlemen, I hope you have had a good trip to China," it read without a hint of irony. "In order to combat H1N1 you will stay at the Fengxian Medical Observation and execution institution for these special days. Stay at your observation room, no come out of your room. This temporary separation is for your family and friends' happiness and health. You will find quality services here. Have a nice time at this special moment."

The Chinese media have reported that travelers placed in quarantine are being held at five-star hotels, but if this is true, then the star system is in need of revision. Imagine a Motel 6 next to a chicken farm in the middle of a field. Then imagine that it had been left abandoned for a year before receiving a quick cleaning and sanitizing and a lot of new security features. The rugs in my room were frayed, and wallpaper peeled from the walls. Mosquitoes abounded. Each room boasted a door alarm that sounded upon opening, and a metal containment fence and police sentries ringed the complex.

I was told that 10 ambulances worked through the night to bring in people from my flight. On my wing of the complex, there were three businessmen, a photographer and her two children, an engineer, a banker and many others. In the days that followed, we were joined by people from other flights.

Discomfort and Isolation

We couldn't leave our rooms, so we passed much of the time standing in our doorways, talking across the empty corridors about the mice, the heat, the food, the missed opportunities, and especially the isolation.

After several days, our frustrations erupted in a series of impromptu rebellions. We attempted to march en masse to the guard station to present our demands: hallway aerobics classes, dinner delivered from a Shanghai steakhouse, better conditions. Each time, the guards eventually coaxed us back into our rooms, and little changed.

But the kind of confinement I experienced flies in the face of established notions of international public health. Quarantine is expensive, and public health needs are many.

Twice daily, three-person medical teams, draped from head to toe in infection-control gowns, caps, goggles, gloves, shoe covers and face masks, visited us to check for fever. Not one of us was ever sick or symptomatic.

After seven days, we were told once again to pack our things. Quarantine-clad observers ushered our haggard group outside and handed each of us a final letter as we waited for chartered buses. "In order to protect public health and keep H1N1 flu from spreading," it read, "we have kept you here for 5-day medical observation."

21

So is China's aggressive approach, which has quarantined thousands of Americans and others, the proper way to protect its population from the new flu?

Poor Strategy for Fighting H1N1

No. Pandemics are serious matters, and quarantines have proved effective in combating the world's most serious contagions, from SARS in the 21st century to the influenza pandemic of 1918.[2] It's understandable that China, which was hit very hard by SARS, would be particularly wary of a new epidemic. But the kind of confinement I experienced flies in the face of established notions of international public health. Quarantine is expensive, and public health needs are many. Most other countries have moved away from quarantine as a means of combating H1N1, in large part because while the virus may yet mutate into a killer infection, it is not considered deadly at present.

The U.S. government recently issued a travel advisory warning travelers about the Chinese government's H1N1 containment efforts, saying there have been reports of "unsuitable quarantine conditions." The internment may have kept us away from Chinese citizens, but it left us vulnerable to getting sick from our quarantine conditions. We were psychologically isolated and disoriented.

China's quarantine policy also has an unpleasant whiff of xenophobia. Chinese passengers were allowed to stay in their homes during the quarantine period instead of being confined to the high-security quarters the rest of us shared. The set-up promoted the narrative that H1N1 was being spread by "foreigners." Quarantined businessmen told me they'd had contracts canceled by their Chinese colleagues, and my Shanghai hotel informed me that my room rate would be triple what it had been if I wished to return.

2. SARS is a respiratory ailment which killed several hundred people in China in 2002–2003. The influenza pandemic of 1918 killed more than 50 million people worldwide.

Many countries—the U.S. included—have tended to see viral illness as coming from "outside," only to learn that pandemics show little respect for national borders in a globalized world. Chinese health authorities need to wake up to this lesson and develop China's ongoing H1N1 response in concert with, rather than in rejection of, international norms.

4

Accusations of Overreacting to H1N1 May Not Be Justified

Effect Measure

Effect Measure is a blog focusing on public health. Its authors are senior public health scientists and practitioners who remain anonymous to allow for freedom of expression.

Mexico instituted strong quarantine measures to slow the spread of H1N1 when the disease first appeared. These measures were controversial and unpopular, but they benefited the world community. Similarly, world and national health officials need to act decisively to combat the disease. If the virus does not cause numerous deaths, this is a sign that efforts to slow it were successful, not that they were unnecessary. Governments and the public need to be careful not to use the claim of "overreaction" as an excuse to downplay future public health crises.

Laurie Garrett of the Council on Foreign Relations and a well-known authority on emerging infectious diseases was on PBS's *Newshour* last night [May 1, 2009] and she made a very important but little appreciated point. Mexico has made a major national sacrifice for global public health by shutting [itself] down . . . and interrupting transmission of disease. The cost to Mexico has already been enormous[, and] it will continue to pay in other ways. The reputation of the government has suffered because of the way it handled this—the lack of transparency, the initial slow-footedness (which of course it denies), its lack of credibility in the eyes of its citi-

Effect Measure, "Swine Flu: The Overreaction Overreaction," May 2, 2009. Reproduced by permission.

zens. There will continue to be a halo of risk and danger for an indeterminate time. And there will be the inevitable backlash against the government's actions, which went from cold to scalding hot in a week. We are starting to see this in the US as well: the "overreaction" backlash. So it's important to sort all of this out. What is the Big Picture at this point?

There is some evidence from 1918 that cities that acted immediately to interrupt transmission by reducing opportunities for contact ("social distancing") did better than those that didn't.

The Spread of H1N1

It's now been a little over a week since swine flu (rebranded H1N1/2009) popped its head above water in southern California. From 2 cases discovered in mid-April in San Diego, the virus is now confirmed to have spread, mostly from Mexico, to 15 countries in North America, Europe and Asia. Confirming a case takes time, so there are significant differences between reports of suspected, probable and confirmed cases, but as of this moment WHO acknowledges 17 deaths (16 in Mexico, 1 in the US) and confirmed 615 cases. The confirmed cases are new, not previously existing but unrecognized cases, and there is clear and convincing evidence of person-to-person transmission. It appears the age distribution continues to be shifted toward younger age groups as compared to endemic seasonal influenza, probably a reflection of the fact that most people are immunologically naive to [that is, they have never encountered] this flu virus. There remains an open question as to whether people who were born before 1957, the date that H2N2 replaced a previous H1N1 as the predominant subtype, may have some cross-reactivity [some immunity] to the current H1N1 strain. In any event, a novel influenza virus has spread quickly worldwide and is transmitting efficiently, pretty much the dictionary definition of a pandemic.

The extent and speed of spread is one factor of concern. The other is the clinical severity of the disease. The good news is that, so far, clinically this influenza virus looks much like a mild seasonal influenza. "Mild" is a relative term. Any influenza infection is a potentially serious disease, and while we have no hard figures, good estimates of the excess mortality caused by influenza yearly in the US is around 35,000 to 40,000. These deaths and the significant but non-fatal illnesses that require hospitalization each flu season are the upper tails, the tip of the iceberg, of flu infections. Most people have milder cases. Some of these "milder" cases are still miserable affairs, with severe headache, joint and muscle aches . . . hacking coughs that can to on for weeks, and malaise and tiredness lasting much longer. Some people are infected and have no symptoms at all. But the more people infected, the more people who are in the upper tail of the distribution. You don't have to shift the distribution much to double or triple the number of people in the tip of the iceberg (think of the tip as a pyramid, and as you raise the iceberg up slightly the new people are in its base, which is much wider). These are the people [who] will stress our already over stressed medical care system. US emergency departments are already over capacity. They would break during a bad flu season.

A Strong Reaction Is Needed

So that's where we are at this moment. There is some evidence from 1918 [when a flu pandemic killed more than 50 million people worldwide] that cities that acted immediately to interrupt transmission by reducing opportunities for contact ("social distancing") did better than those that didn't. We would of course expect this on common sense grounds as well. That's what Mexico has done—and I echo Laurie Garrett's point, they have done so at great cost [to themselves but] to everyone's benefit. That is what is behind CDC's [Centers for Disease Control and Prevention] recommendations that a school be closed as soon as a case is confirmed. There is a cost to that, too. Proms are canceled, to the deep disappointment of the [promgoers] and the economic loss of the venues and ancillary businesses. Exams are delayed. Child care needs for younger students produce a ripple effect throughout the community. And as in Mexico, these costs can produce a backlash if the public doesn't understand why they have been incurred.

The irony is that the overreaction backlash will be more severe the more successful the public health measures are. If, for example, the virus peters out this spring because transmission was interrupted long enough for environmental conditions (whatever they are) to tip the balance against viral spread, CDC and local health officials will be accused of overreacting. It's another example of the adage, "When public health works, nothing happens." On the other hand, if local officials do nothing and things get worse, they will be accused of being slow.

If there is an overreaction to perceived overreaction, the job of rationally preparing for a plausible near-future event will be made much more difficult.

Do Not Become Complacent

It's not just the current reputation of local officials that concerns me, however. If this virus does wane with the summer months (something we expect to happen), its current mildness and its disappearance may lead citizens and decision makers back into the kind of reckless disregard of public health facts that has produced our current weak and brittle health infrastructure. But flu season will come again next fall, and it would be no scientific surprise if this strain is part of flu's repertoire. Most of the world would still be unprotected unless we spend the interim preparing for the possibility it will reappear in a more serious clinical form (flu viruses are notorious for that kind of change). When I say prepare, I am not [talking about just] a vaccine, although that will be an important, but difficult part. We will also need to invest urgently in a health care, public health and social infrastructure to absorb the consequences of potentially large-scale absenteeism. We will also need to work out policies that will allow social distancing measures to work (child care, sick leave policy and other issues).

It's an urgent task that must be started immediately. If there is an overreaction to perceived overreaction, the job of rationally preparing for a plausible near-future event will be made much more difficult.

5

Calling H1N1 "Swine Flu" Unfairly Damages Pork Producers

Brian McVicar

Brian McVicar is a reporter for the Grand Rapids Press.

H1N1 cannot be caught from pigs. However, based on the fact that the H1N1 virus was called "swine flu," many people avoided pork, causing serious problems for hog farmers. Government leaders called on the media to stop using the term "swine flu," but even with that help, hog prices have been down and farmers have faced a harsh economic market.

Few names bug hog farmer Ross Brink as much as the one that burst onto America's radar in spring: Swine flu.

The 26-year-old Allegan County [Michigan] hog farmer has an ax to grind with whoever coined swine flu, a term for the H1N1 influenza virus.

Hog Farmers Face Numerous Challenges

He says the link has contributed to less demand for pork.

"I think people just get scared when they hear the words 'swine flu,'" said Brink, whose family owns Seldom Rest Hog Farms in Overisel Township [Michigan]. "People think the food's unsafe and the meat's unsafe."

It's a tough time to be a hog farmer, and it's not just swine flu causing the problem, experts say.

Brian McVicar "Unfounded H1N1 Fears, Based on 'Swine Flu' Name, Hurts Pork Business, West Michigan Hog Farmers Say," Mlive.com, November 11, 2009. Reproduced by permission of Grand Rapids News.

Many hog farmers are being squeezed by high feed prices, the slumping economy, decreased global demand and the risk of their hogs of catching swine flu.

H1N1 cannot be caught from eating pork, according to the CDC.

"It's extremely tough times," said Sam Hines, executive vice president of the Holt-based Michigan Pork Producers Association.

"I've been in the industry 50 years, and I've never seen anything as bad as now."

When it first emerged, the H1N1 virus was believed to have originated in pigs. Studies for the federal Centers for Disease Control and Prevention have identified genes from human, bird and pig viruses.

H1N1 cannot be caught from eating pork, according to the CDC.

Still, some people have still shied away from buying pork, Hines said.

"It did reduce demand," he said. "When the virus was first identified back in the spring, we even got calls here from people wondering whether it was safe to consume pork they had in their freezers."

Congress Asks Media Not to Use "Swine Flu"

The fears became so widespread that U.S. Agriculture Secretary Tom Vilsack in September called on the news media to stop using the term swine flu. He said the name has upset markets and pork producers.

"It's just as easy to say H1N1 as it is to say swine," he said.

Reduced demand, caused in part by the link to the influenza virus, has hurt pork producers at home and abroad, according to an Oct. 1 [2009] letter signed by 24 U.S. senators, including Sen. Debbie Stabenow, D-Mich.

As a result, the nation's pork industry has lost an estimated $53 million per week and farmers have taken a $21 loss on each hog, according to the letter sent to Vilsack.

At his 2,000-acre farm where his family sells about 10,000 hogs a year, pigs are fetching about $105 each. That is $20 less than it costs to raise one.

The senators also are asking the government to purchase an additional $100 million of pork for federal food programs and work with federal agencies to help address swine disease surveillance on farms.

The financial hardships have caused farmers like Brink to tighten their belts.

At his 2,000-acre farm where his family sells about 10,000 hogs a year, pigs are fetching about $105 each. That is $20 less than it costs to raise one.

"You try to ride the storm out," Brink said. "When times are good, you save and pile it away for when times are bad."

Still, the situation has not been easy.

"That's roughly a $20 loss per pig we're shipping out," he said. "That adds up over the course of the year."

The high price of feed is hurting hog farmers, too.

As production of corn-based ethanol increased in recent years, so did the demand for corn, which many hog farmers use for feed.

High demand was caused in part by 2005 federal legislation mandating 7.5 billion gallons of renewable fuels such as ethanol be mixed with gasoline by 2012.

Corn prices hit what Hines called an all-time high of around $8 a bushel—56 pounds—in summer 2008.

Prices have since declined, but they're still higher than a few years ago, he said. A bushel of corn now runs $3.83.

Nailing a market strategy has been tough for many pig farmers, including Bob Dykhuis, of rural Holland [Michigan].

He sells about 7,000 hogs a week from farms spread throughout Southwest Michigan and north-central Indiana.

"It's been a confusing market," Dykhuis said. "There's so many external factors."

Shrinking global demand has been chief among them, he said.

Following the April [2009] H1N1 outbreak, demand for pork dropped in several markets. Those included Mexico and China, the latter of which recently lifted a ban on U.S. pork imports that began shortly after the outbreak, according to the National Pork Board.

6

H1N1 Should Be Called Swine Flu

Seth Borenstein

Seth Borenstein won the National Journalism Award for environment reporting in 2007 from the Scripps Foundation. He is a science writer for the Associated Press; a news agency owned by its American newspaper and broadcast members.

The World Health Organization (WHO) has stopped using the term "swine flu," claiming the term was misleading and caused pig slaughter in some countries. The name "swine flu" has caused a stigmatization and had negative results on the pork industry. "Swine flu" is a scientifically accurate name, in that the virus is related to viruses that develop in pigs, and therefore should remain the name of the 2009 H1N1 virus.

No matter what you call it, leading experts say the virus that is scaring the world is pretty much all pig. So while the U.S. government and now the World Health Organization are taking the swine out of "swine flu," the experts who track the genetic heritage of the virus say this: If it is genetically mostly porcine and its parents are pig viruses, it smells like swine flu to them.

Six of the eight genetic segments of this virus strain are purely swine flu and the other two segments are bird and human, but have lived in swine for the past decade, says Dr. Raul Rabadan, a professor of computational biology at Columbia University.

A preliminary analysis shows that the closest genetic parents are swine flu strains from North America and Eurasia, Rabadan wrote in a scientific posting in a European surveillance network.

"Scientifically this is a swine virus," said top virologist Dr. Richard Webby, a researcher at St. Jude Children's Research Hospital in Memphis. Webby is director of the WHO Collaborating Center for Studies on the Ecology of influenza Viruses in Lower Animals and Birds. He documented the spread a decade ago of one of the parent viruses of this strain in scientific papers.

. . . the WHO said it would stop using the name swine flu because it was misleading and triggering the slaughter of pigs in some countries.

"It's clearly swine," said Henry Niman, president of Recombinomics, a Pittsburgh company that tracks how viruses evolve. "It's a flu virus from a swine, there's no other name to call it."

Dr. Edwin D. Kilbourne, the father of the 1976 swine flu vaccine and a retired professor at New York Medical College in Valhalla, called the idea of changing the name an "absurd position."

The name swine flu has specific meaning when it comes to stimulating antibodies in the body and shouldn't be tinkered with, said Kilbourne, 88.

That's not what government health officials say.

"We have no idea where it came from," said Michael Shaw, associate director for laboratory science for the Centers for Disease Control and Prevention. "Everybody's calling it swine flu, but the better term is 'swine-like.' It's like viruses we have seen in pigs, it's not something we know was in pigs."

On Wednesday, U.S. officials not only started calling the virus 2009 H1N1 after two of its genetic markers, but Dr. Anthony Fauci the National Institutes of Health corrected reporters for calling it swine flu. Then on Thursday, the WHO said it would stop using the name swine flu because it was misleading and triggering the slaughter of pigs in some countries.

Another reason the U.S. government wants to ditch the swine label is that many people are afraid to eat pork, hurting the $97 billion U.S. pork industry. Even the experts who point to the swine genetic origins of the virus agree that people can't get the disease from food or handling pork, even raw.

"Calling this swine flu, when to date there has been no connection between animals and humans, has the potential to cause confusion," Chris Novak, chief executive officer of the National Pork Board, said in a news release.

One top flu expert, doesn't like the swine flu name either, but for a different reason. Traditional swine flu doesn't spread easily among people, although this one does now, said Dr. Paul Glezen, a flu epidemiologist at Baylor University.

Columbia's Rabadan said sometimes when he talks to other scientists, he uses the name "swine" or the name "Mexican flu." And that name only adds another case of political incorrectness.

Mexico Health Secretary Jose Angel Cordova said it's wrong to call it "North American flu" and flatly rejects the idea of calling it "Mexican flu." He pointed to WHO information that the swine genes in the virus are from Europe and Asia. Rabadan and others say four of the six pure swine genetic markers are North American.

"I don't think it's fair for someone to blame Mexico for this. You can't blame any country; you can't blame a person or an institution. The recombination of genes in the virus is something that happens naturally," Mexico's chief epidemiologist, Miguel Angel Lezana said Wednesday.

And while the U.S. government and WHO are dropping "swine flu" as the name, someone hasn't told their Webmasters.

On Thursday afternoon, the phrase "swine flu" was still in the Internet addresses for the WHO, Homeland Security and CDC pages on the disease and the question-and-answer page on the U.S. government's pandemic flu Web site.

7

The H1N1 Vaccine Is Safe

Joseph Albietz

Joseph Albietz is an assistant professor of pediatrics at the University of Colorado, Denver, and The Children's Hospital. He is an associate editor at the blog Science-Based Medicine.

According to the best scientific evidence as of December 2009, the H1N1 vaccine appears to have no dangerous side effects. On the other hand, the 2009 H1N1 flu appears to be significantly more deadly than the usual flu strains. Because the flu is dangerous and the vaccine is safe and effective, people, and especially children, should get vaccinated.

We are nearing [as of December 2009] the end of the second wave of the 2009 H1N1 pandemic, and are now a few months out from the release of the vaccine directed against it. Two topics have dominated the conversation: the safety of the 2009 H1N1 influenza vaccine, and the actual severity of the 2009 H1N1 infection. Considering the amount of attention SBM [Science-Based Medicine, the blog for which this viewpoint was written] has paid the pandemic and its surrounding issues, and in light of a couple of studies just released, it seems time for an update.

2009 H1N1 Vaccine Safety

This week the CDC [Centers for Disease Control and Prevention] released a report that evaluated the safety record of the 2009 H1N1 vaccine. The first two months of the vaccine's use

Joseph Albietz, "An Influenza Recap: The End of the Second Wave," Science-Based Medicine, December 11, 2009. Reproduced by permission of the author.

were examined, from October 1st through November 24th, using data from two of the larger surveillance systems monitoring the 2009 H1N1 vaccine's safety: the Vaccine Adverse Event Reporting System (VAERS) and the Vaccine Safety Datalink (VSD). This report represents the largest, and to date best, evaluation of the 2009 H1N1 vaccine's safety profile since its initial testing and release. The findings are reassuring.

We've talked about VAERS' uses (and abuses) in the past. Nevertheless, used properly as a surveillance tool, a "canary in a coal mine," it can be quite helpful. In that two-month span of time when 46.2 million doses of H1N1 vaccine were distributed, 3,783 adverse events associated with it were reported to VAERS; 204 of these events were classified as "serious," including 13 deaths that occurred within 19 days of vaccine administration.

At first blush people may assume (unwisely) that the vaccine directly caused each of these reported events, and would thus yield an adverse event rate of 82 total adverse events and 4.4 serious adverse events per 1 million doses. This is indeed the assumption (and mistake) made by people claiming for instance that the flu vaccine has caused X number of deaths or Y cases of Guillain-Barré syndrome (GBS) [a nervous system disorder resulting in weakness and paralysis, sometimes linked to vaccines]. Even taken (again, unwisely) at face value, these rates would be impressively low, particularly when compared to the risks of H1N1 infection, as we shall see later.

Indeed, considering the population's baseline mortality rate, it's remarkable that only 13 people out of 46.2 million died within 3 weeks of receiving the vaccine by chance alone.

The story is even more reassuring once we look properly at the data. It bears repeating that VAERS does not (nor was it meant to) establish causation, it only holds the potential to suggest a correlation. We should also bear in mind that GBS, death, all adverse events in fact, occur at a baseline rate in the population in the absence of the vaccine (a hypothetical vaccine causing *zero* adverse events would still have a list of adverse events reported to VAERS, reflecting the population's baseline rates). Thus to even determine if there is a significant correlation between the vaccine and any given adverse event, we need to determine not only how many adverse events occur in relation to the 2009 H1N1 vaccine, but the number that occur *above the expected baseline*.

That having been said, let's examine the most concerning number first, the 13 reported deaths. . . . There is no discernable pattern to the ages of these unfortunate people, their underlying diseases, or their causes of death. Nine of these 13 people had *significant* underlying diseases, and one of them died in a car accident. Indeed, considering the population's baseline mortality rate, it's remarkable that only 13 people out of 46.2 million died within 3 weeks of receiving the vaccine by chance alone. This doesn't definitively exonerate the 2009 H1N1 vaccine from these deaths (well, we can probably safely rule out the car accident), but it certainly makes its involvement highly unlikely.

The VAERS database provides no reason to suspect the 2009 H1N1 vaccine has anything but chance correlation with cases of GBS [Guillain-Barré syndrome].

H1N1 Vaccine, GBS, and Other Adverse Events

What of the concern [about] Guillain-Barré syndrome (GBS) following vaccine administration? After all, at least one influenza vaccine [administered in 1976–77 in the U.S.] in the last three decades has been shown to cause GBS in rare cases, and some poorly handled stories in the media have further elevated public concern.

The first two months of vaccine use saw 12 cases of suspected GBS reported to VAERS. Investigation into these reports has confirmed 4 of these to be cases of GBS, 4 were not GBS, and the final 4 are still under scrutiny.

Again, these cases require context. As the baseline rate of GBS is $\sim$ [up to] 1/100,000 people per year, $\sim$550 cases can be expected to occur in the US during the two months of this report. [The incidence of these] 8 likely cases of GBS in 46.2 million doses of vaccine is certainly not higher (and is in fact far less) than what one would expect to see by chance. The VAERS database provides no reason to suspect the 2009 H1N1 vaccine has anything but chance correlation with cases of GBS.

There is no correlation between the H1N1 vaccine and either GBS or death, but what of other concerning adverse events? An evaluation of the 204 serious events reported reveals a scattershot of diseases, none of which have a signal that rises above baseline rates.

The CDC report contains a similar analysis using data from the VSD, [in which] 438,376 doses of the H1N1 vaccine had been administered and adverse events tracked. As with the VAERS data, no serious adverse events rose above their baseline rates.

The 2009 H1N1 has thus far claimed the lives of at least 250 children in between the traditional flu seasons, which is more than the two prior flu seasons combined.

In short, after the first two months of use and 46.2 million doses, the VAERS and VSD data fails to provide any evidence to correlate the 2009 H1N1 vaccine to any serious adverse event. Given the seasonal influenza vaccine's similar record over the past several decades, that the 2009 H1N1 vaccine continues to display an exemplary safety profile is not unexpected, but it is reassuring.

The Severity of 2009 H1N1

What of H1N1's severity? What toll has it exacted? The CDC has made detailed information, updated weekly, available to the public on its Fluview website. Containing a wealth of information, [Fluview can let you] see 2009 H1N1's unique and peculiar epidemiology, the unseasonable spikes in outpatient visits for influenza-like illnesses that have troubled our EDs [emergency departments] for the last few months, and the trend of lab-confirmed influenza hospitalizations and mortality over time.

Hard numbers are also available. As of November 28th, at least 31,320 people in the US have been hospitalized and 1,336 have died from 2009 H1N1 since August 30th. The 2009 H1N1 has thus far claimed the lives of at least 250 children in between the traditional flu seasons, which is more than the two prior flu seasons combined.

This data is most helpful if viewed as the minimum confirmed impact of the disease, and as a catalogue of the most severe cases to date. What you will not find on the Fluview site is the actual incidence of influenza infection, the total number of people infected, including minor infections. This number is extremely valuable when trying to gauge the true severity of any infection, but fiendishly difficult to acquire.

A study published in [the online journal] *PLoS Medicine* this week [December 2009] contains one of the latest attempts to quantify 2009 H1N1's severity to date. Drawing from the data of two US cities during the initial wave of infections between April and July [2009], they estimated that of all 2009 H1N1 infections . . . 0.16%–1.44% will require hospitalization, 0.028%–0.239% will require ICU care, and 0.007%–0.048% will die.

This study has garnered a significant amount of attention, for its estimates of severity are considerably lower (thankfully) than those made by the President's Council of Advisors on Science and Technology in early August [2009]. The accuracy

[of] and differences between these estimates, [plus] the inherent difficulty of determining the true incidence, severity, and future course of diseases like influenza [warrant a separate] post, and I'll not address this particular angle in greater depth here.

I'd like to [reflect instead] on what these two studies might tell us about the risks of contracting 2009 H1N1 compared to the risks of receiving the vaccine to protect against it.

The Virus Is More Dangerous than the Vaccine

On the one hand, we have a virus that has proven itself to be widespread and highly contagious, to have claimed the lives of at least 1,336 and hospitalized over 30,000. Conservative estimates from the PLoS study place one's risk of hospitalization if infected at ~1/625, and risk of death ~1/14,285. Furthermore, though we have completed the second wave of the pandemic, a third wave is almost certain to come. A small minority of the population has thus far been infected, past influenza pandemics have featured a triple peak, and we have now entered the beginning of the traditional influenza season.

Please, particularly if you or yours are in a high-risk group, get vaccinated.

On the other hand, we have an inexpensive vaccine which is an excellent match to this strain, generates an appropriate antibody response in most people (particularly those in the highest risk groups for 2009 H1N1), and after [more than] 46 million doses has yet to be significantly correlated with any severe adverse events.

There are still a lot of uncertainties regarding the rest of this influenza season. Will we have a third peak of H1N1, and if so, how severe will it be? Will it continue to preferentially afflict the young, or will the elderly suffer a greater impact than they have to date? How will the presence of 2009 H1N1 impact the normal flu season—will it be cumulative, or will 2009 H1N1 "crowd out" the seasonal strains? The list goes on, and it absolutely includes the possibility that with ongoing surveillance and studies we may identify a serious but rare side effect caused by the vaccine.

As time goes on we will continue to refine our knowledge of influenza, and these questions will be answered, but it is unlikely that the big picture will significantly change. Influenza is a virus with serious potential for harm that can be prevented by one of the safest interventions in modern medicine. Please, particularly if you or yours are in a high-risk group, get vaccinated.

8

The H1N1 Vaccine Is Not Safe

LeM22

LeM22 is a teacher from northern Virginia who writes on Hubpages.

The 1976 H1N1 flu vaccine resulted in deaths and incidences of Guillain-Barré syndrome, a neurological disorder. The current 2009 H1N1 vaccine has been rushed into production without being sufficiently tested. In addition, the drug companies that developed the vaccine have been granted legal immunity from lawsuits. Given these conditions, parents should be very careful about inoculating their children with H1N1 vaccine.

During the past 100 years, the H1N1 virus has hit Americans twice that we know of, and possibly three times if you include the 1918 epidemic [that killed more than 50 million people worldwide, and] which some scholars and scientists attribute to the swine flu.

The swine flu was originally an influenza virus that was passed amongst pigs; hence the name *swine*. It is very common among pigs; it is very rare among humans. Very rarely does it pass between animal and human. That's the good news. The bad news is that once it does, the original strand, like any virus, may mutate and lead to new strains of the virus. The bad news continues when it is remembered that by the time drug manufacturers create a vaccine for a certain strain of the virus, it is usually outdated.

As children head back to school in the coming months, the chances of a renewed outbreak will be heightened. Currently, the swine flu is not as invasive as it normally would be because children are not "indoors" as much as they will be in a few days. Secondly, most adults are outdoors much more, contributing to a reduction in the number of cases verified. Yet, there are five clear reasons why the H1N1 flu shot should not be taken in mid-October [2009] when it becomes available for the first time.

The Dangerous 1976 Flu Vaccine

Of all the influenza outbreaks in our recent (100 year) history, the swine flu virus has been the leading cause. The 1918 "Spanish" flu was actually the H1N1 virus that mysteriously spread as the war was ending, and then [was] conveniently carried home to the soldiers' native lands. This effectively spread the virus to the entire world at the end of World War I. Renamed "the Spanish flu," (because neutral Spain provided the world with most of the information about it) the virus killed . . . 50–100 million people worldwide, most of them healthy and young. Reports indicate that it started in the United States . . . in southern military bases, and was carried over to the trenches as America entered and ended the war.

The 1976 swine flu vaccination killed more people than the virus itself.

The 1976 outbreak started with a soldier in Fort Dix, New Jersey. The virus quickly took on the name of the neurological condition that the vaccine inculcated: Guillain-Barré.

The current viral outbreak began near the border of Mexico, location unknown.

The 1976 swine flu vaccination killed more people than the virus itself. Whoa! After a young private died, medical authorities ascertained that 500 other military personnel had become infected and had fully recovered. Yet, the CDC [Centers for Disease Control and Prevention] and [Gerald] Ford presidency decided upon a policy of mass inoculation that resulted in hundreds dying and contracting the Guillain-Barré disorder.

Even though some testing is being conducted, it is neither thorough [nor] complete.

The swine flu has traditionally singled out young people. Most of them come down with symptoms that imitate a "mild flu" virus. Consequently, the vaccine is targeted towards children for this fall [2009]. Depending on your understanding of the flu, and what you believe to be the cause or reason [for] it, a very difficult decision is presented to those with children. The targeted population will be at highest risk at the time the vaccination is made available. As with the timing of the 1918–19 epidemic, the timing of this outbreak appears to be at its worst when children are coming back from their summer breaks and spending more time inside due to the colder weather in our hemisphere. Anything that targets our youth is a cause of concern for everybody.

More Testing Is Needed

Due to the coming school year, the government is concerned that the virus will spread and infect up to 40% of the population. They have decided to skip the normal testing protocol in order to provide the vaccinations by mid-October [2009].

Even though some testing is being conducted, it is neither thorough [nor] complete. And, it will not be finished before the vaccine is made available. Currently many family physicians are not jumping on the federal bandwagon and, "harbor doubts about safety of the vaccine or the danger the flu poses . . . children in particular should not be asked to bear the burden of being experimental subjects. . . ." [according to a November 8, 2009 article in the *Washington Post*]

Another concern is the activating agents that are used within the vaccine itself. These "boosters" will result in more of the vaccination being made, but have dangerous side effects. These boosters have been banned by the FDA for all vaccinations, but are being allowed for the current production of the swine flu virus.

Many analysts question the role that vaccinations play in the development of ADHD [Attention Deficit Hyperactivity Disorder], autism, and other neurological disorders in children.

The drug companies and government have now received legal immunity, so that if there are any problems, side effects, or deaths, they cannot be sued. Seeing how the pharmaceutical companies will receive billions out of the fall vaccination program, it is equally stunning that they will receive immunity from all lawsuits. This means that there is no recourse if you choose to receive a swine flu shot. You will have to accept all consequences, for better or for worse.

9

Obama Is Responsible for the Inadequate Response to H1N1

Michael Eden

Michael Eden is a conservative blogger at the site Start Thinking Right.

The Obama administration has mishandled the production of H1N1 vaccine. As a result, there are vaccine shortages that may result in numerous deaths and serious economic hardship as people stay home for fear of contracting the virus. Because of its liberal bias, the media is not holding the administration responsible. The administration's incompetence shows that the government should not be allowed to pass health reform and take a greater role in the health care system, however.

Remember when President [Barack] Obama "declared a national emergency to deal with the 'rapid increase in illness" from the H1N1 influenza virus.' Boy, did they ever get the ball rolling after *that*.

Vaccine Shortages

Even as it became increasingly obvious that the administration was falling woefully behind in [its] H1N1 production goals, they continued to urge people to demand the vaccine. The result was more typical of Soviet-era breadlines than the U.S.A.

Not only am I not able to get this stupid vaccine, but both my doctor and my dentist have told me that *they* aren't able to get it, either.

Michael Eden, "H1N1 Vaccine As Proof of Mind-Boggling Obama Incompetence," Start Thinking Right, November 17, 2009. Reproduced by permission.

Even *The New York Times* pointed a finger at Obama last month [October 2009] in an article entitled . . . "H1N1 Widespread in 46 States as Vaccines Lag":

Federal officials predicted last spring that as many as 120 million doses could be available by now, with nearly 200 million by year's end. But production problems plagued some of the five companies contracted to make the vaccine. All use a technology involving growing the vaccine in fertilized chicken eggs; at most of them, the seed strain grew more slowly than expected. . . .

The Obama government predicted 120 million doses, but—as the article makes clear—they have only 30 million. This is an absolute disaster—and it is entirely appropriate to compare this level of sheer incompetence to George [W.] Bush's "Katrina moment." [which refers to the Bush Administration's inadequate response to Hurricane Katrina in 2005 and the way it damaged his presidency.]

Are conservatives wrong to blast Obama for this gross incompetence?

And blaming the delays that will leave Americans woefully exposed to H1N1 is tantamount to George Bush blaming the Hurricane Katrina response on the American Red Cross. That pig just doesn't fly, Barry Hussein. [Obama's middle name is Hussein.]

Swine Flu Dangers Grow

This [report from Bloomberg.com] is not good:

Swine flu, also known as H1N1, may infect as much as half of the population and kill 30,000 to 90,000 people, double the deaths caused by the typical seasonal flu, according to the planning scenario issued yesterday by the President's Council of Advisors on Science and Technology. Intensive care units in hospitals, some of which use 80 percent of their space in normal operation, may need every bed for flu cases, the report said.

A revised report from the CDC [Centers for Disease Control and Prevention] dated November 12 [2009] demonstrates that all the kings horses and all the king's men really don't have a whole lot of a clue as to what is going on:

> Federal health officials now say that 4,000 or more Americans likely have died from swine flu—about four times the estimate they've been using [according to a CBS/AP story].

If you go back and survey this slowly unfolding disaster, you will find that the Obama government has routinely been wrong by a factor of . . . 400%–500%. At some point you'd think the mainstream media would really start coming unglued over this incompetence. But not so much (hint: the president is a *Democrat*).

The fact that the Obama administration assumed control of the flu vaccine in an unprecedented way makes Obama and the Democrats even more blameworthy.

Are conservatives wrong to blast Obama for this gross incompetence?

Not if history counts for anything (which it usually doesn't with liberals). Amy Geiger-Hemmer [of the blog *It's Hemmer Time*] writes:

> Remember a few short years ago how President [George W.] Bush was just ripped apart by the mainstream media and blamed for flu vaccine shortages? Most Democrat representatives acted outraged at the President and his inability to have enough flu vaccines available for the American people during flu season. . . .

And that was just an ordinary flu year. No "national emergencies." No super-flu. No flu that kills four times as many people as authorities predicted it would.

Not that Democrats (and that includes the mainstream media) are capable of being fair or objective, but if they were only capable of turning their demagoguery on themselves . . .

Obama's Incompetence May Cause Deaths

This is not only a shocking failure, but an incredibly dangerous and potentially deadly failure as well:

> "I'm worried the virus (H1N1) is getting ahead of the public health system's ability to control it"—Senator Joe Lieberman

And the fact that the Obama administration assumed control of the flu vaccine in an unprecedented way makes Obama and the Democrats even more blameworthy yet [according to John G. Winder of *The Cypress Times*]:

> There are extreme shortages of the H1N1 vaccine all over the U.S. As a result, people are getting sick and they are dying. This pandemic is raging, and spreading like wildfire, and for the first time ever the private sector has been removed from the process of distributing the vaccine.
>
> It has been standard operating procedure in the past for private industry to distribute vaccines that were needed for the greater good of the people. Now, however, with the H1N1 vaccine and the Obama administration in charge, the government has taken over all responsibility for distribution of the vaccine to the states via the CDC. The government has failed so miserably in distributing the vaccine that now the [Democrat!!!] U.S. Senate is investigating [for evidence of] incompetence and possible corruption. . . .

We're talking about the worst kind of incompetence. . . .

And the [question] that the Democrat candidate for president [John Kerry] asked in 2004 applies big time now: "If you can't get flu vaccines to Americans, what kind of health care program do you think you can run?"

Are you going to allow these clowns to run your health care system? Are you going to trust them with your life? Are you going to put another [fifth] of the economy under their control? [The Obama Administration in 2009 was attempting to pass a health care reform package that would give government more control over health care.]

[You] are aware that many retail businesses make 70% of their profits during the Christmas season? What happens if people are afraid to shop for fear of the H1N1 Obama Death?

Speaking of the economy, this isn't merely a health disaster; it is increasingly likely that it will create a massive economic disaster as well.

[You] are aware that many retail businesses make 70% of their profits during the Christmas season? What happens if people are afraid to shop for fear of the H1N1 Obama Death?

Consider that what is increasingly likely to become a health disaster is even *more* likely to be an economic disaster, as H1N1 escalates its attack during the holidays and the Christmas shopping season, with still no significant stocks of vaccine available.

How much longer can Obama keep blaming Bush for his growing list of failures?

10

U.S. Pharmaceutical Firms Are to Blame for the H1N1 Vaccine Shortage

Tom Eley

Tom Eley is a writer for World Socialist Web Site.

The shortage of vaccines in October 2009 was caused by the fact that creating vaccines is not profitable for large companies. As a result, many U.S. companies did not make vaccines despite the dangers of H1N1. The lack of vaccines thus shows that corporations cannot be entrusted with public health. In addition, the situation exposes the weaknesses of the world health system, in which less developed countries lack vaccines, and of the U.S. health system, which is seriously unprepared to deal with a flu pandemic.

Vaccines against the H1N1 virus are unavailable to tens of millions who need the inoculation in the United States, the result of the failure of major pharmaceutical corporations to deliver them as promised.

Not Enough Vaccine

The H1N1 virus, popularly known as swine flu, has already infected millions and claimed the lives of more than 5,000 worldwide and at least 1,000 in the US, with a much higher death rate than typical flu strains. The swine flu is now epi-

Tom Eley, "Obama Declares US National Emergency over H1N1 Flu," World Socialist Web Site, October 26, 2009. Reproduced by permission.

demic in 46 states. The lack of the vaccine, which may not be available in sufficient quantity for months, will result in more deaths and serious illnesses.

President [Barack] Obama declared a national state of emergency Saturday [October 24, 2009], which allows state and local governments to set up emergency inoculation facilities and hospitals to waive normal rules for the distribution of vaccine. This follows the more limited declaration of a public health emergency last April 26 [2009], when the new flu strain first became widespread in Mexico.

The declaration underscores the current problem: inadequate medical facilities are being mobilized to distribute even more inadequate supplies of the vaccine.

The major pharmaceutical corporations tasked with making available vaccines in tens of millions of doses have come up far short. The Obama administration had anticipated that by the end of October [2009], 40 million doses would be available. Instead, as of Wednesday [October 21, 2009], a mere 11.3 million had been delivered to health care providers, according to the Centers for Disease Control [and Prevention] (CDC), with only 16 million expected by the end of the month.

"We are nowhere near where we thought we'd be by now," CDC Director Thomas Frieden said in a Friday press briefing. "We are not near where the vaccine manufacturers predicted we would be. We share the frustration of people who have waited online or called a number or checked a Web site and haven't been able to find a place to get vaccinated."

The production of flu virus vaccines is hampered by antiquated technology. Currently, vaccines are created by growing viruses in chicken eggs, a cycle that normally takes between six and nine months. The prediction that the swine flu vaccine would be broadly available at the end of October [2009] was based on the assumption that vaccine manufacturers could produce large quantities on the shorter end of the cycle.

Novartis AG's production of the vaccine has been one fifth of what [the company] anticipated, the result, it says, of a surprisingly low yield using the egg method. The Swiss-based pharmaceutical contracted with the US government to produce 90 million doses. Novartis officials now say they will not be able to meet that goal until the end of the year [2009], meaning that there will likely be a shortage of the vaccine until January [2010] or beyond.

The private corporations' failure to come even close to meeting social need for the H1N1 vaccine exposes the official myth of the profit system's supposed infallibility in allocating economic resources.

Vaccines Are Not Profitable

The fact that an old and time-consuming method is used in the production of vaccines is not only a technical problem. Major pharmaceuticals find the production of vaccines to be insufficiently profitable. Vaccines do not realize high profits on the market, and, moreover, after one flu season an entire year's production has exhausted its usefulness and must be thrown out. Some firms eschew making vaccines altogether; it is noteworthy that of the five pharmaceuticals contracted to supply the American market, none is US-based and only one has US production facilities.

The US pharmaceutical industry would have plenty of resources to invest in the development of technology for flu vaccines if [it] desired to do so. The annual revenues of [drug company giants] Merck and Pfizer, for example, dwarf the $53 billion turnover for Novartis.

There is also evidence that the companies contracted to produce the swine flu vaccine did not adequately invest in new production lines. Bruce Gellin, director of the National Vaccine Program Office of the US Department of Health and

Human Services, spoke of "brief interruptions in operations" in this regard, according to *The Wall Street Journal.*

One company, MedImmune (a subsidiary of the Anglo-Swedish AstraZeneca PLC), which contracted with the US to produce 40 million vaccine doses, is on target with its production, about half of which has been of the nasal spray variety of immunization. But the distribution of these vaccines has been hampered by a lack of the sprayers to deliver the inoculation, the *Journal* reports.

The private corporations' failure to come even close to meeting social need for the H1N1 vaccine exposes the official myth of the profit system's supposed infallibility in allocating economic resources. Where social need fails to coincide with the profit imperative, as in the mass production of vaccines, the "invisible hand" [which guides the market according to philosopher Adam Smith] simply fails.

The Poor Will Suffer Most

Efforts to fight the spread of the swine flu are further complicated by the lack of a coherent, coordinated global strategy. Instead, each national government has adopted its own plan—or done nothing at all—with the wealthier nations effectively cornering the global vaccine market.

> *The emergency declaration also demonstrates the administration's fear that failure to provide the vaccine to those in need could provoke widespread social anger.*

The population of the so-called developing world—the majority of humanity—must wait and see if there are any leftovers after the wealthier nations have had first call. The Obama administration has said it will donate what remains unused of the H1N1 vaccine to poor countries—hardly a magnanimous gesture, given that the remainder would otherwise be thrown in the garbage.

The H1N1 epidemic has exposed the existing social order in another way. This year has seen a wave of layoffs and hiring freezes by state and local public health agencies, a result of the [late-2000s] economic crisis that has dramatically cut tax revenue. Coming after decades of policies that have starved public health—and virtually eradicated state hospitals—there is little infrastructure in place in the US to handle epidemics. It is this factor that is particularly exposed in Obama's declaration of a national emergency

The emergency declaration also demonstrates the administration's fear that failure to provide the vaccine to those in need could provoke widespread social anger. "Officials are mindful that the previous administration's failure to better prepare for and respond to Hurricane Katrina in 2005 left doubts that dogged President George W. Bush to the end of his term," *The New York Times* reports.

The vaccine shortage has already led to long lines at vaccination centers around the nation. Some of those in need have even camped out in the hope that they will get the inoculation.

The swine flu has thus far preyed mostly on children and adolescents. But even those with compromised immune systems—the frail elderly, those with AIDS, and pregnant women—have largely been unable to get the vaccine.

"I thought I'd be a priority, being nine months pregnant," Mary Kate Merna told the *Times* at lineup for the vaccine in Chicago. She arrived too late. Pregnant women are about six times [the national average] more likely to die . . . if they contract the swine flu.

Free clinics to administer the swine flu vaccine in Chicago drew thousands on Saturday, most of whom were turned away. "Workers at the Truman College clinic reported that the line started at 7:30 A.M.—90 minutes before the clinic opened," the *Chicago Sun Times* reported. "By 10:30 A.M., the last of 1,200 yellow numbered cards was handed out, which meant all of the day's vaccine was accounted for."

"Even with a declaration of an emergency, it doesn't mean anything unless you have a vaccine," Health and Human Services Director Zachary Thompson of Dallas, Texas, told a local news station. "We don't need the 20,000 doses at the end of November [2009]—we need the 20,000 now."

The CDC expects that the swine flu will pass through the population in what it called a series of "waves" over the coming months. It is not clear how deadly it will prove to be. Most of those who contract the disease have fairly mild symptoms. However, the relatively high flu death toll prior to the onset of the normal flu season has raised widespread concern, among both health care professionals and the broader public.

11

The U.S. Must Address Systemic Failures in Its Own Health System

Bob Graham and Jim Talent

Bob Graham is a former Democratic senator from Florida. Jim Talent is a former Republican senator from Missouri. They are respectively chairman and cochairman of the Commission on the Prevention of Weapons of Mass Destruction Proliferation and Terrorism.

The U.S. response to H1N1 exposed the inadequacy of outdated health systems for diagnosing viruses, tracking their progress through the population, and developing vaccines. Yet, despite this inadequate response, the United States is far better prepared to deal with a flu outbreak than with a biological terrorist attack. Because such an attack is likely in the near future, the United States must update its health system quickly to deal with both natural and synthesized threats.

For generations, the United States has neglected to nurture the technologies and systems needed to respond to emergencies related to disease. Nowhere has this been more evident than in the response to H1N1.

Outdated Systems

To make flu vaccine, we rely on a 60-year-old production method based on chicken eggs. It is safe but slow and has led to long lines at clinics and shortages of vaccine. It is not just

Bob Graham and Jim Talent, "H1N1 Response Shows Need for Better Medical Emergency Plans," *Washington Post*, January 4, 2010. Reproduced by permission of the Commission on the Prevention of Weapons of Mass Destruction Proliferation and Terrorism.

that priority groups have been left unprotected. We learned last month that this method leads to multiple manufacturing issues, such as the recall of 800,000 children's vaccine doses, due to diminished potency.

Our nation relies on a disease surveillance system that doesn't give useful information about an epidemic, such as the severity of illness, transmission rates and spread of disease in communities. Even today, we have no idea how many people have had the H1N1 virus. If this country had an up-to-date system, we could make better decisions about school closings, infection control guidance and antiviral drug use.

In short . . . America's experience with H1N1 shows that the nation is not prepared to deal with a flu pandemic.

We also rely on an outdated, slow method for diagnosing cases of H1N1. Our diagnostic technologies are difficult, expensive and time-consuming. If rapid tests were available, people who are sick could get treatment sooner, and we could determine the size of an outbreak, whether the disease is getting more severe and how to target limited health resources.

In short, despite the tireless efforts of public health and health-care workers, America's experience with H1N1 shows that the nation is not prepared to deal with a flu pandemic.

The really bad news is that we are far more prepared to respond to a flu outbreak than to any other biological event[— natural or synthesized—]such as the Ebola virus [a deadly virus that can be transmitted through body fluids].

In six to nine months last year [2009], the United States was able to identify this new H1N1 virus, make vaccine and begin distributing it, though in inadequate amounts. There is no other disease to which our public health infrastructure could respond anywhere near as quickly. For most new diseases, the response time would be more like six to nine years.

Biological Terror Attacks Would Be Worse

We are the leaders of the congressionally mandated Commission on the Prevention of Weapons of Mass Destruction Proliferation and Terrorism, which found in 2008 that it was not just possible but probable that terrorists would succeed in using a weapon of mass destruction somewhere in the world by 2013 and that the weapon would most likely be biological. We can anticipate the likely pathogens terrorists would use, but this information is meaningless if we do not have the stockpiles, medical countermeasures and tested plans for distributing them to affected areas. Terrorists will not give us six months' warning before deploying a biological weapon.

The major review that Secretary of Health and Human Services Kathleen Sebelius announced recently for our nation's capabilities for developing and distributing countermeasures is a step in the right direction. But this must happen quickly, and it is only the beginning of the journey to full preparedness.

As bad as H1N1 has been for affected families, it could have been much worse.

The good news is that science has the means to develop and stockpile countermeasures to known pathogens, and to vastly improve our capacity for responding to new diseases. Unfortunately this will not happen through private-sector action alone, and our government, including the last several administrations, has not given this issue the consistent priority it deserves.

If the planned review is simply a sporadic response to the high visibility of H1N1, or to the repeated and highly public warnings by our commission, it will result in yet more talk without action. The H1N1 epidemic will subside and be forgotten, and our commission will go out of business in the spring. But the danger, both natural and [synthesized], will grow.

As bad as H1N1 has been for affected families, it could have been much worse. It could have been a human-to-human transmissible form of H5N1 [also known as avian flu], which could kill up to 70 percent of those infected. It could have been an anthrax or Ebola attack on a major city, which could expose several million people to deadly pathogens.

We don't know how to repeat our warning or our recommendations more plainly: In the judgment of our bipartisan commission, such an event is not only possible but likely; and it could result in the death of a few people or hundreds of thousands, depending on whether our government develops the complete chain of response, including links for surveillance, diagnosis, stockpiles of medical countermeasures and effective distribution networks.

We know from the attempted airplane bombing on Christmas Day [2009, when a terrorist attempted and failed to ignite an explosive device] that al-Qaeda is a determined enemy. We also know—from the discovery and dismantling of biological weapons labs in Afghanistan—that they are pursuing biological weapons research.

The necessary investment of public funds is relatively modest. What has been in short supply is leadership. The announced review is a good first step. But will real action follow, and will it happen in time?

12

The World Must Address Systemic Failures in the Global Health System

Peter Navario and Scott Rosenstein

Peter Navario is a fellow in global health at the Council on Foreign Relations. Scott Rosenstein is a global health analyst in Eurasia Group's comparative analytics practice.

Most H1N1 vaccine stocks were available to industrialized nations but not to the developed world. This is inhumane and inequitable. It also threatens the developed nations, since if disease takes hold in developing nations, it may mutate and spread to other regions. In addition, the developing world may not cooperate in disease prevention if it sees itself being treated unfairly. For reasons of humanity and self-interest, therefore, the developed world needs to put systems in place to ensure vaccine is available in the developing world.

Much of the domestic discourse on preparedness for the second wave of H1N1 has focused on the speed with which a vaccine has been produced, which ignores a striking fact: ninety percent of H1N1 vaccine stocks will be distributed to individuals in the U.S. and eleven other wealthy countries, while the rest of the world must make due with the remains.

As the 95 poorest countries wait for vaccine donations from the U.S. and elsewhere to arrive, which will . . . allow them to vaccinate just two percent of their populations, the Netherlands has begun to sell off surplus vaccine stock. This inequality in access has sparked criticism from public health and human rights advocates, who argue that there is an epidemiologic and moral imperative to ensure vaccine availability in poor countries. Though these criticisms may be valid, they fail to address a more politically persuasive point that lack of access to vaccinations in low- and middle-income countries imperils domestic public health and national security. Ad hoc vaccine sharing is not only an incomplete strategy for managing global health threats . . . it also leaves the U.S. population vulnerable.

The majority of vaccines (including H1N1), as well as essential medical supplies such as face masks and ventilators, are manufactured abroad.

There are several reasons [that] it is in the interests of the U.S. to enhance global vaccine access and pandemic response capacity in low- and middle-income countries. First, the current vaccine allocation arrangement ensures that countries with the least capability for managing a pandemic also have the least access to life-saving vaccines and medicines, thereby perpetuating the cycle of illness and poverty in poor countries, and creating fertile ground for new or re-emerging viruses to replicate, mutate and eventually spread back to the U.S.

Moreover, during a more virulent outbreak, the U.S. could be exposed to broader economic risks due to disruptions to the "just-in-time" global economy. In 2003, the poorly managed SARS [a respiratory infection that killed hundreds in China and elsewhere] outbreak halted travel and trade in Southeast Asia and cost an estimated $50 billion in that region alone.

Finally, the majority of vaccines (including H1N1), as well as essential medical supplies such as face masks and ventilators, are manufactured abroad. A severe pandemic with high rates of illness and death could lead to rampant absenteeism from work, or worse, hoarding in countries that produce and manufacture these goods. The risk of hoarding is increased if there is a persistent perception that wealthy countries act according to narrow self-interest during global health emergencies. Unfortunately, this has already happened. Indonesia has refused to share virus samples and report cases of the deadly H5N1 [avian] flu virus to the World Health Organization (WHO) for fear that wealthy countries would use this information to produce costly drugs and sell them back to poor countries at a profit. While the reasoning is severely flawed and endangers the health of people all around the world, it reveals the potential consequences of persistent inequality in access to essential medicines.

The world needs a formal governance mechanism for pandemic emergencies that procures, stockpiles and distributes vaccines and supplies for developing countries to replace the current system of ad hoc donations.

More Vaccine, Better Surveillance

The H1N1 experience has taught us that a more robust U.S. response must address the inadequate global supply of vaccine during pandemic emergencies, often called "surge capacity," and enhance low- and middle-income countries' domestic response capabilities.

Work on expanding the supply and domestic production capacity is under way, and the U.S government should continue to support newer production approaches, such as cell-based or DNA-based vaccines, which can help to mitigate current surge capacity shortfalls. To complement these efforts, the U.S. FDA should expedite the review of safety and efficacy data of adjuvant-boosted vaccines [ones containing adjuvant ingredients, which increase a medication's effectiveness]. Adjuvants serve as a multiplier, exponentially increasing the number of people who can be immunized by a given amount of vaccine, and they have been extensively tested and used in Europe and Canada safely for years. Contrary to the spurious rhetoric from the anti-vaccine movement, adjuvant use in the U.S. would enable the demand for domestic vaccine to be met rapidly and safely. It would also enhance our ability to supply vaccine to poorer countries.

In addition to stimulating vaccine production, the U.S. should devote additional financial and technical resources to building disease surveillance and response capacity in developing countries. Most importantly, the world needs a formal governance mechanism for pandemic emergencies that procures, stockpiles and distributes vaccines and supplies for developing countries to replace the current system of ad hoc donations. The G7 [a group of Finance Ministers from seven industrialized nations] plus Mexico recently met to discuss equitable vaccine distribution; the [U.S.] should ensure that such a mechanism is part of ongoing discussions.

H1N1 will not be the last or worst pandemic humanity will face. [The disease] should therefore serve as a "teachable moment" for the U.S. and other donor nations. Poor countries' inability to manage pandemic emergencies poses a threat to health everywhere. International solidarity on pandemic management, guided by enlightened self-interest, is not only the right thing to do and good foreign policy, it is essential to ensuring the health and security of the U.S. citizenry.

13

Wal-Mart's Sick Leave Policy May Contribute to the Spread of H1N1

National Labor Committee

The National Labor Committee (NLC) is an organization de-voted to defending the human rights of workers. It investigates and exposes human and labor rights abuses committed by U.S. companies producing goods in the developing world.

Wal-Mart has a punitive sick-leave policy, which docks pay and issues demerits when an employee is forced to stay home from work because of sickness or family emergency. This policy en-courages employees to come to work sick for fear of losing wages or even of being fired. As a result, Wal-Mart employees with the flu might come to work and infect coworkers and shoppers, even as their children might attend school sick and infect other chil-dren. Wal-Mart's policy directly contradicts Centers for Disease Control and Prevention recommendations, and it should be changed immediately.

Punishing workers for taking sick leave puts Wal-Mart on track to be a major spreader of swine flu this fall [2009]. The retail giant gives workers demerits and deducts pay for staying home when they are sick or to care for a sick child.

Working While Sick

In interviews with Wal-Mart "associates" at stores across New York State, employees confirmed that they had no choice but to work sick. One Wal-Mart employee from a supercenter ex-

National Labor Committee, "Wal-Mart's Sick Leave Policy Risks Spreading Swine Flu," November 3, 2009. Reproduced by permission.

plained: "*Plenty of girls are coughing their brains out. But they cannot go home because of points. Everyone comes in sick. You can't stay home, and God forbid if you leave early.*" "Associates"—including food handlers working in the grocery, meat and even deli departments—are routinely coming to work with the flu, conjunctivitis, fevers, strep throat, diarrhea and vomiting. It is only when an employee is coughing too loudly and violently that he or she will be transferred from the food section to another department, where the sick worker will still be interacting with customers.

An experienced worker at a Wal-Mart discount store similarly confirmed that "*people are coming in sick all the time.*" In fact, just last week several cashiers at her store came to work with flu-like symptoms, only staying home when they were so sick it was impossible for them to work. (The most contagious period for swine flu is at the beginning of the illness.)

The Centers for Disease Control and Prevention (CDC) is strongly recommending that employers "*advise workers to be alert to any signs of fever and other signs of influenza-like illness before reporting to work every day, and notify their supervisors and stay home if they are ill.*" The CDC goes on to recommend that "*business and other employers should prepare to institute flexible workplace and leave policies for their workers.*" The CDC alerts employers to "*expect sick employees to be out for about 3 to 5 days in most cases, even if anti-viral medications are used.*" Further, "*Employers should maintain flexible policies that permit employees to stay home to care for an ill family member. Employees should be aware that more workers may need to stay home to care for ill children or other ill family members than usual.*"

Wal-Mart's policies routinely flout [defy] the CDC's recommendations, putting both associates and shoppers at risk.

Another Wal-Mart associate told us, "*Wal-Mart won't even look at a doctor's note. If you are out sick, you're going to get a demerit and lose eight hours' wages.*" The H1N1 virus, or swine flu, is known to spread from person to person when those infected cough or sneeze, propelling virus-carrying droplets into the air that can be inhaled by people in the vicinity, and onto surfaces like countertops that customers touch.

Wal-Mart has a punitive point (demerit) system that punishes workers who cannot come to work because they are ill or their children need care.

On October 1, 2009, Ken Senser, a senior vice-president for Wal-Mart, distributed a memo nationwide on "Flu Season Preparation" to all Wal-Mart associates. Wal-Mart associates were told to *"cover your nose and mouth with a tissue when you cough or sneeze," "wash your hands regularly,"* and *"avoid touching your eyes, nose or mouth."*

Not a single word was said about the critical CDC recommendation that workers with *"any signs of fever and other signs of influenza-like illness . . . stay home if they are ill."* Instead, Mr. Senser goes on . . . *"familiarize yourself with relevant company policies, including those for attendance, sick pay and return to work following an illness."*

Punished for Being Sick

But Wal-Mart's policies on sick leave are the problem. Wal-Mart has a punitive point (demerit) system that punishes workers who cannot come to work because they are ill or their children need care. Associates who miss a day due to sickness (or for any other reason) will receive a one point demerit, along with the loss of eight hours' wages. Moreover, employees who *"have more than three absence occurrences in a rolling six-month period . . . will be disciplined."* Workers with four absences in any six-month period—no matter what the reason—will be disciplined. A fifth occurrence—like a sick day—will result in *"active coaching"* by management, and a sixth occurrence" will activate a *"Decision Day,"* when an "associate" can either be terminated or put on a year-long trial period, during which a worker can be fired for any infraction, no matter how insignificant. During this year-long probation, the worker cannot receive a promotion.

This is the reason Wal-Mart employees must drag themselves to work no matter how sick they are. Not only due to the fear of termination, but with associates typically living from paycheck to paycheck, they cannot afford the loss of eight hours wages.

Single mothers working at Wal-Mart are under particular stress. In September [2009], an associate received a call from her four-year-old's pre-school, telling her to come pick up her child, who had a fever of 103 [degrees] F. Despite the fact that she had worked four hours, for leaving work to pick up her child she received a point and lost the rest of the day's wages. Parents have no choice but to load their children up with Motrin and Dimetapp to mask their symptoms so they can go to school.

In his memo, the senior vice-president advised Wal-Mart associates to "*have back-up childcare plans in the event your child cannot attend school.*" Here too, Wal-Mart ignores the CDC's recommendation that employers "*be prepared to allow workers to stay home to care for children if schools are dismissed or childcare programs are closed . . . Ensure that your leave policies are flexible and non-punitive.*"

Asked about Wal-Mart's "family-oriented policy," another employee bluntly stated: "That is in the toilet. They don't care about families."

This fits Wal-Mart's longstanding business model of externalizing and outsourcing as many costs as it can. Rather than developing affordable healthcare, Wal-Mart assists its associates in enrolling their children in state-supported Child Health Plus/Medicaid programs. Rather than taking responsibility to follow the CDC's recommendation that employers adopt flexible leave policies so that parents can stay home with their sick children, Wal-Mart advises its associates to *"have back-up childcare plans in the event your child cannot attend school."* This leaves associates to scramble on their own to find family members or relatives who can take time off to watch their children, or to find a babysitter willing to do this.

This led a Wal-Mart employee to note that, *"Even during the flu season, Wal-Mart wants to be first, and our children's health and schooling comes second."* Another associate, a young mother, said: *"It makes you feel horrible. Wal-Mart puts you in a position where you are supposed to put your job ahead of your children."*

Asked about Wal-Mart's "family-oriented policy," another employee bluntly stated: *"That is in the toilet. They dont care about families."*

Wal-Mart Policies Contradict CDC Recommendations

I. Sick Employees Punished for Staying Home:

Any Wal-Mart employee with swine flu or other serious communicable illnesses will be punished if they stay home, receiving a point (demerit)—five or six points can lead to termination—and incurring the loss of eight hours wages.

Wal-Mart's policy on "authorized absences" does not cover sick days, including for those suffering from the H1N1 virus. To avoid punishment, employees would have to apply for a sick day *"at least three weeks in advance,"* which is, of course, ridiculous. *"Requested time away from work which has been approved by your supervisor or manager and included in the schedule at least three (3) weeks in advance is not considered an absence."* Even with a request made three weeks in advance, there is no guarantee that the day off will be granted.

In Wal-Mart-speak, taking a sick day is referred to as an "*occurrence*": "*Occurrence means any time away from scheduled work that is not approved by your supervisor or manager as . . . set forth in this Policy,*"—which, again, does not recognize sick days as an "*authorized absence.*"

Wal-Mart employees live in fear that the next family emergency will result in their being fired.

Unauthorized absences apply not only to sick days, but also to days workers must take off to care for a sick child or elderly parent, because of school closings, car accidents, snowstorms, preventative medicine such as getting blood work done, attending a funeral for a nephew, and so on. Each "occurrence" results in the worker receiving a point. "*If you have three occurrences in a rolling six-month period, you will have the opportunity to discuss your absences with management during a personal discussion. If you have more than three absences in a rolling six-month period, you will be disciplined.*" Workers can be terminated when they receive five or six "occurrences"—demerits—in any six-month period. Wal-Mart employees live in fear that the next family emergency will result in their being fired.

Not only do Wal-Mart employees receive a point if they are out sick, they also lose their wages. "*You must wait one scheduled workday before using your available Illness Protection pay. An additional waiting period is required for each separate absence. . .*" This means that even workers who have accrued paid sick time cannot use it and will be docked eight hours pay for each new sick day they must take.

The potent combination of punitive demerits and the loss of wages for taking a sick day—even if one is suffering from the swine flu—routinely drives sick Wal-Mart employees to work, where they are in a position to spread their illness to other workers and customers.

Moreover, Wal-Mart employees who are out sick for more than three days must apply for a Leave of Absence. *"If you will be absent for more than three days, you should submit a completed Request for Leave of Absence form. You should submit the required documentation for approval to your supervisor. Requesting leave of absence does not automatically assure the leave will be approved. Please refer to the Leave of Absence Policy (PD-24) for additional information."*

This means Wal-Mart employees who may have the H1N1 virus, and are being advised by the CDC to remain at home for three to five days until they are symptom free, must file for a Leave of Absence, which will include getting a note from a doctor, which the CDC views as a waste of precious time, given the work load doctors are facing during the current epidemic.

While the CDC advises employers to allow their employees to remain home to care for sick children, Wal-Mart instructs its employees to *"have back-up child care plans in the event your child cannot attend school."*

Rather than allow—let alone encourage—Wal-Mart employees to stay home to care for their young children who may have H1N1 influenza, or because of school closings due to the current epidemic, Wal-Mart places a further burden on its employees by instructing them to make arrangements so that other people can care for their children.

Wal-Mart Policies Endanger Employees and Shoppers

During this swine flu pandemic, Wal-Mart's policies, in every important way, ignore and contradict CDC recommendations, thereby placing its own employees and Wal-Mart shoppers at risk.

When the largest private employer in the U.S. sets the wrong example in the fight against the H1N1 pandemic, the American people should take notice

Wal-Mart is the largest private sector employer in the U.S., with 1.4 million employees in 4,258 stores across the country. In New York state alone, Wal-Mart has 109 stores and 37,784 employees. With its tremendous size and sales reaching $401 billion (in the fiscal year ending January 31, 2009), Wal-Mart services more than 150 million shoppers each week.

Wal-Mart shoppers, employees and their families are being put at risk when senior Wal-Mart executives ignore and contradict critically important [CDC] guidelines meant to control and prevent the spread of swine flu, which is already widespread in 48 states.

During this swine flu pandemic, Wal-Mart's policies, in every important way, ignore and contradict CDC recommendations, thereby placing its own employees and Wal-Mart shoppers at risk.

Wal-Mart must immediately end its punitive point system, which gives workers demerits that can lead to firing for taking a sick day, while also docking their wages. More than any other Wal-Mart policy, it is the point system and loss of wages which routinely drives employees to work no matter how sick they are, including if they are suffering flu-like symptoms.

Wal-Mart employees feel it is completely unjust that management automatically deducts the first eight hours wages of any sick day or leave, especially given how hard they must work to accrue paid sick leave. A Wal-Mart employee must work 40-hour weeks for an entire month to accrue just 4 hours of sick leave. As one worker put it: *"It's our money and we worked hard to earn it. It's not right that we can't use our own money to cover sick days."*

The vast majority of current Wal-Mart employees are too terrified to speak openly and on the record, or even to name their stores [for] fear of retaliation. *"Everyone knows you have to be quiet,"* as one associate put it, *"We can't talk. Everyone is afraid and will never say anything critical*" of Wal-Mart. A senior Wal-Mart employee agreed: "*Fear and need will keep things as they are.*"

Another point of consensus that we heard from Wal-Mart workers across New York State is that: "*Everyday shoppers have no idea what is really going on at Wal-Mart.*"

Centers for Disease Control and Prevention Recommendations on H1N1

I. "Sick persons should stay home"

- "*One of the best ways to reduce the spread of influenza is to keep sick people away from well people.*"

- Employers should "*advise workers to be alert to any signs of fever and other signs of influenza-like illness before reporting to work each day, and notify their supervisor and stay home if they are ill.*"

- "*CDC recommends that employers with influenza-like illness remain at home until at least 24 hours after they are free of fever (100 degrees or greater) or signs of a fever, without the use of fever-reducing medications.*"

- Employers should "*Expect sick employees to be out for about 3 to 5 days in most cases, even if anti-viral medications are used.*"

- Employers should "*Ensure that your sick leave policies are flexible and consistent with public health guidance and employees are well aware of these policies.*"

- "*Do not require a doctor's note for workers who are ill with influenza-like illness to validate their illness or to return to work, as doctors offices and medical facilities may be extremely busy and may not be able to provide such documentation in a timely way.*"

- *"Employers should maintain flexible policies that permit employees to stay home to care for an ill family member. Employers should be aware that more workers may need to stay at home to care for ill children or other family members than is usual."*

- *"People at higher risk for complications from influenza include pregnant women; children under 5 years of age; adults and children who have chronic lung disease (such as asthma), heart disease, diabetes, diseases that suppress the immune system and other chronic medical conditions, and those who are 65 years [old] or older."*

II. Taking Care of Sick Children

- Employers should *"be prepared to allow workers to stay home to care for children if schools are dismissed or childcare programs are closed."*

- Employers should *"ensure that your leave policies are flexible and non-punitive."*

14

Forcing Businesses to Offer Paid Sick Leave Is Not an Answer to H1N1

Michael B. Enzi

Mike Enzi is a Republican U.S. senator from Wyoming.

U.S. President Barack Obama's administration has badly fumbled the H1N1 response. In the absence of needed vaccine, small businesses have developed innovative policies to confront the illness. This shows that businesses will formulate better health care policies than can be handed down by government. Furthermore, unfunded government initiatives will hurt small businesses in a time of economic crisis, causing job losses. Therefore, Congress should not impose a nationwide sick-leave policy.

Today [November 10, 2009] Americans across the country are trying to protect themselves and their families from the threat of the flu pandemic that is threatening the lives of children and pregnant women around the world. Yet when they show up at the doctor they are being told that there [is no more vaccine] and that, due to shortages in supply, they will have to be put on a waiting list until the next shipment arrives. . . . They are learning that their government has failed to prepare the country for the threat of a flu pandemic that was foreseeable and preventable with better coordination and preparedness.

Michael B. Enzi, "The Cost of Being Sick: H1N1 and Paid Sick Days," in United States Senate, November 10, 2009.

Poor Preparation

The 2009 H1N1 virus was first detected in Mexico in March of 2009 and a month later in the U.S. Today it is widespread in 48 states, including my home state of Wyoming, yet most Americans who want to protect themselves by vaccination have been left in the lurch, and told that a supply of vaccines may not even be available before the pandemic is over.

This summer [2009] the Administration [of U.S. President Barack Obama] promised Americans that 80 to 120 million doses of the vaccine would be distributed by mid-October. Yet, here we are a month past the deadline and only 36 million doses are available.

As for the doses that are available, the Administration appears to be taking inadequate precautions to ensure fair and appropriate distribution. The media is full of stories of vaccines going to populations that don't fit the high risk profile—such as terrorism suspects being held at Guantanamo Bay—instead of those populations at risk, such as small children and . . . pregnant women.

With death tolls rising and almost no access to the vaccine, it is no wonder that we are concerned. Every person left unvaccinated is an opportunity for H1N1 to spread exponentially and mutate into a more deadly strain. I'm pleased that we have a representative of the [Centers for Disease Control and Prevention] here today to shed light on what has gone wrong and to tell us what improvements can be made.

I also want to welcome Dr. Scott Gottlieb . . . today to discuss some of the policies that have contributed to the vaccine shortage, and provide recommendations for ways to improve our response to pandemic flu in the future.

Increase Preparedness

Some of these issues include the decision at the Department of Health and Human Services (HHS) to order single dose instead of the more efficient multi-dose vials. Multi-dose vials are produced more quickly, and can out-produce single-dose vials 10 to 1. We have also yet to approve the use of adjuvants [ingredients that increase the effectiveness of a medication] in flu vaccines, which decrease[s] the amount of the vaccine needed in a single dose—which would allow us to vaccinate more people with the same amount of vaccine. Adjuvants are currently used in the flu vaccine sold in Europe but are not yet approved for use in flu vaccines in the U.S.

What works in one place of business may not work in another; and what we inflexibly mandate may not be best for all.

Another shortfall we face is regarding the production process. Today, the U.S. still depends on chicken eggs for their vaccine production, while other nations are using more advanced cell-based manufacturing processes that are not dependent on a supply of eggs and can more quickly increase vaccine production. One way that the federal government can improve our production capabilities is through increases in funding for the Biomedical Advanced Research and Development Authority (BARDA). We also need to approve the cell-based manufacturing process for the flu vaccine so that manufacturers will not need to wait for FDA approvals the next time our nation faces the threat of pandemic flu. It is imperative that the U.S. increase its capabilities to produce better technology that will increase our preparedness capabilities in the future.

Today's hearing will focus on the impact that H1N1 has on sick and healthy Americans every day. But let us not lose sight of the opportunity for Congress to learn from this experience and continue to force our nation to increase our preparedness capabilities. The alarm that the H1N1 virus has raised in many households also translates to our workplaces. Employers recognize that an outbreak of the epidemic among their employees could shut down a business for weeks or longer, and, in the absence of widespread access to the vaccine, they are taking steps to protect their employees. They are providing information about flu prevention, hand sanitation tools and similar products, preparing for telecommuting and running their operations with smaller staff. One of today's witnesses, Ms. Elissa O'Brien, will testify about her company's vigorous H1N1 flu prevention efforts. Her company has also adopted a leave policy which generously provides a starting level of 26 days of paid leave and short term disability coverage—enough to accommodate the flu needs of every employee—but which would be upended if the one-size-fits-all Healthy Families Act[1] became law. Reading through her testimony, I was reminded that Washington [D.C.] does not have a monopoly on good ideas; and that whenever we act prescriptively, we also decrease flexibility and creativity. What works in one place of business may not work in another; and what we inflexibly mandate may not be best for all.

Business Finds Better Solutions

As we all remember, the Healthy Families Act bill was a heartfelt priority of our late Chairman, Senator [Edward] Kennedy. Before I entered public service I was a small business owner, so I am speaking from experience when I say the goal of the legislation is something we all share. In a small business, employees are like family members. Employers know that if they want to attract and keep good employees they must give them the flexibility they need [to] care for their own health and their loved ones. Indeed, in the most recent member benefit survey conducted by the Society for Human Resource Management, some 86% of the respondents reported that their companies provided paid sick leave either under a separate sick leave program, or as part of a general paid time off plan.

---

1. The Healthy Families Act of 2009 was a bill introduced to Congress that would require businesses to provide up to seven days of paid sick leave per year.

Over 80% of the respondents also indicated that they provide both short-term and long-term disability insurance coverage; and an increasing number utilize even more creative approaches such as paid time off, and sick leave banks, or pools.

Hitting small businesses and start-ups with new costs and unfunded mandates is never advisable, and it is even more irresponsible during a time when job creation should be a top priority.

The beauty of these creative approaches is that they are responsive to the needs and wants of employees, the changing costs of providing different benefits, and the ability of the employer to provide the benefits while staying in business. In contrast, the type of leave mandated by this and similar bills . . . is completely inflexible. It also would add to the practical problems human resource officers deal with every day by importing intermittent leave and medical verification rules, which have proven problematic in other statutes. In addition, this bill provides no deterrents for abuse of the leave entitlements and raises privacy concerns—two issues that employers have found innovative ways to resolve in the absence of a mandate.

Most employers provide sick-leave benefits both because they know that a healthy workforce benefits their business, and because they know that in a competitive labor market they must address this issue to attract and retain quality employees. Today, the average cost of employee benefits for all employers in the private sector is nearly $8.02 an hour. Average benefits now [total] 30% of total payroll costs. While the number of employers finding ways to provide paid leave as part of their benefit package continues to increase, there are some employees who do not have paid sick leave available to them at their place of work. The bulk of these individuals are employed by smaller employers who, especially in challenging times like these, are struggling to maintain current payrolls.

And that is getting harder and harder. Friday's [November 6, 2009] job numbers showed we lost another 190,000 jobs last month [October 2009] and the unemployment rate reached a 26-year high of 10.2 %. Hitting small businesses and start-ups with new costs and unfunded mandates is never advisable, and it is even more irresponsible during a time when job creation should be a top priority.

Imagine the irony for an employee who is granted sick leave under this bill, but whose employer decides to eliminate or reduce health plan benefits.

Balance Jobs with Health Care

It is a simple fact: whenever we impose unfunded mandates on employers, the money necessary to pay those increased costs must come from somewhere. No matter how desirable the goal, one cannot simply dismiss the cost as unimportant or inconsequential. Here, the costs are decidedly not inconsequential, particularly for smaller businesses. The pool of available labor dollars is not infinite, and when we mandate their expenditure for a specific purpose, we always run the risk of unintended consequences, such as adding to the growing pool of unemployed workers. A dollar that must be spent here, often results in a dollar that will not be spent elsewhere. Imagine the irony for an employee who is granted sick leave under this bill, but whose employer decides to eliminate or reduce health plan benefits.

The H1N1 pandemic has raised concerns for Americans looking to protect themselves and their families, as well as for employers seeking to keep their businesses going and their employees healthy. These concerns, however, are layered on top of the economic worries that have recently plagued us, and the unemployment numbers which continue to rise. Now more than ever, we should be lifting up America's small businesses to help create economic growth and to create sustainable jobs. This is not the time to compound the problems small businesses are facing with another unfunded, inflexible mandate from Washington.

15

Canada Needs to Update Federal Statutes to Respond to H1N1

Lloyd Duhaime

Lloyd Duhaime is the senior partner of the Vancouver law firm Duhaime Law. He writes on the Web site Duhaime.org.

Canada has no effective national law to deal with public health emergencies such as swine flu. There is no uniform duty to report cases of infectious disease and no standard quarantine policy. Neither does the law in general allow the use of the criminal code as stopgap measure to detain those who are infectious. Canada desperately needs to pass national statutes to deal with contagious diseases, or an epidemic will result in many unnecessary deaths.

Pigs are, well, pigs.

They like their home in disarray; *aka*, a pig sty.

It should then come as no surprise to Canadians to discover that the law in regard to the swine flu, more commonly known as H1N1, is a statutory pig sty, a disaster itself.

In modern times, the first brush Canada had with infectious or communicable disease was HIV and AIDS, [with] which tens of thousands of Canadians are now infected. SARS [a respiratory infection which was centered in China] killed 44 Canadians in 2003.

Lloyd Duhaime, "H1N1 Law—Swine Law for a Swine Flu," Duhaime.org, November 6, 2009. Reproduced by permission.

Intermittently, there have been small outbreaks of communicable diseases and, in the result, there is a quilt of disparate and knee-jerk law from coast to coast dealing with this critical, essential and national public-health issue.

Canadians find to their horror that there is no cohesive national statutory response to communicable disease.

They can't even agree on basic terminology.

The federal government, in its Quarantine Act, prefers *communicable disease*.

Jocelyn Downie, in *Canadian Health Law and Policy*, and the World Health Organization (WHO), prefers *infectious disease*.

Canadians find to their horror that there is no cohesive national statutory response to communicable disease.

Why professional hockey players can receive a vaccine while infants and pregnant women must wait, is simply opportunism in the face of a vacuum of the effective law.

Can't blame hockey players.

They average six feet, two inches and they are all wealthy.

In anarchy, whole or partial, the tough, the rich and the elite always do well.

Duty to Report

The first inkling of law [that] arises with a communicable disease such as H1N1 is usually the duty to report.

The good news is that every Canadian jurisdiction requires reporting of cases of specified communicable diseases.

But only some jurisdictions require schoolteachers or hotel keepers to report. Consider the novelty of $[section]22(1) of the 2008 Alberta *Public Health Act*:

Where a health practitioner, a teacher or a person in charge of an institution knows or has reason to believe that a person under the care, custody, supervision or control of the health practitioner, teacher or person in charge of an institution is infected with a communicable disease prescribed in the regulations for the purposes of this subsection, the health practitioner, teacher or person in charge of an institution shall notify the medical officer of health of the regional health authority. . . .

In some provinces, it is only the name of the infected individual that has to be reported—not his or her address, as if a name without an address is going to do a health officer any good.

There is little guidance given to medical doctors as to when they disclose the *who* and *where* in the event of discovery of a highly communicable and dangerous disease.

In the background looms the ethical codes of all Canadian doctors that, unless specifically required by law, they must not divulge patient information without consent.

In 2009, in the BC [British Columbia] *Venereal Disease Act*, doctors are warned at §12, that they "must preserve secrecy about all matters that come to the person's knowledge in the course of the person's employment". If they do otherwise, "a person who defaults in (this) duty . . . must forfeit the person's office or be dismissed from the person's employment"!

The doctor is put to the unenviable choice: "Shall I save lives or keep my daughter in private school?"

Contacts, Detaining, and Quarantine

Reasonably (duh!), some public health statutes require that a communicable disease be followed up by notifying persons who came into contact with the infected person.

However, this is . . . mandatory [only] in some provinces. Others, like Newfoundland and Alberta, merely say that contacts *may* be notified, at the discretion of the public health officer.

Generally, most jurisdictions authorize the medical health officer to arrange for the detention of a person with a infectious disease, but that is where the statute homogeneity ends.

Some [such as Québec and Prince Edward Island] require a court order signed by a judge.

Other jurisdictions, such as under the Ontario *Health Protection and Promotion Act*, set up a small initial circus where[in] the senior politician orders the person to conduct himself in such a manner so as not to expose another person to infection.

If he or she does not do so, the patient may then be detained.

Sure; like time is not of the essence and we can rely on self-policing.

There is no solid, uniform statute on quarantine in Canada. However, the federal government has enacted a Quarantine Act for incoming travelers. Finally, something sensible and national:

> A quarantine officer may detain any traveler who . . . the quarantine officer has reasonable grounds to believe has or might have a communicable disease . . . or has recently been in close proximity to a person who has or might have a communicable disease or is infested with vectors, and is capable of infecting other people.

The quarantine powers include, in select jurisdictions only (Québec and Prince Edward Island, for example), the power to close down any place which has become a beehive of [that is, swarming with] the infectious disease, such as a school.

Newfoundland—God bless them—has opted to take the bull by the horn; §31 of their Communicable Disease Act:

> Where the minister is of the opinion that a communicable disease is epidemic or threatens to become epidemic in a community, he or she shall have authority to issue an order, declaring the disease epidemic, and to order and enforce

those measures in the way of quarantine, isolation of the sick, vaccination, disinfectant, closing of schools, public or private or prohibition of public gatherings that in his or her judgment may be necessary to stamp out the infection or contagion.

That's why we pay taxes, for that kind of political leadership.

There is a sprinkling of cases that deal with quarantine. In *City of Toronto v Deakin*, Justice [Bruno] Cavion had before him a person "recalcitrant" with his tuberculosis. The Province wanted to quarantine Wayne Deakin, and Deakin wanted to be left alone, citing the Charter of Rights and Freedoms.

Cavion blessed the use of force against Deakin:

> . . . shackling was never vindictively or arbitrarily applied.
> . . . (D)octors and staff . . . are handling a most difficult and
> challenging situation with wisdom and sensitivity. . . . I find
> the occasional use of restraints was necessary and limited.

---

*National swine flu law is, in effect, nonexistent. There
are no effective weapons in the national lawmaker's armory to withstand these lethal forces of nature.*

The Criminal Code

Canada's *Criminal Code* is not the knight in shining armour one might expect in this void of a national statute on communicable diseases generally, and the swine flu in particular.

In *Chambers v BC*, the British Columbia Court of Appeal ruled that the *Criminal Code* could not be used for civil enforcement purposes, including communicable diseases, short of criminal conduct. Justice [Patricia] Proudfoot:

> It was not the intent of Parliament that the Criminal Code
> be used to confine persons who may develop . . . communi-
> cable disease.

But, §180 and §221 sound great on paper:

> Every one who commits a common nuisance and thereby endangers the lives, safety or health of the public . . . is guilty of an indictable offence and liable to imprisonment for a term not exceeding two years.

> Every one who by criminal negligence causes bodily harm to another person is guilty of an indictable offence and liable to imprisonment for a term not exceeding ten years.

In *R v Thornton*, the accused knew he had AIDS and that he was infectious. . . . [T]his turkey still gave blood to the Red Cross, but it was screened and discarded. Thornton was charged under §180 of the Criminal Code. Justice Galligan stated the obvious:

> Throughout this century and indeed since much earlier times, the common law has recognized a very fundamental duty, which while it has many qualifications, can be summed up as being a duty to refrain from conduct which could cause injury to another person.

National swine flu law is, in effect, nonexistent

There are no effective weapons in the national lawmaker's armory to withstand these lethal forces of nature.

The pressing need for a strong and effective national statute or uniform legislation on contagious disease is not rocket science, and yet here we are, in the midst of the most dangerous public health influenza in decades, languishing in a crumbling patchwork of provincial laws.

It's public health anarchy, which results in avoidable death and from which, if we do not learn, death returns in the next wave.

16

America Does Not Need More Statutes to Respond to H1N1

Ed Richards

Ed Richards is a Harvey A. Peltier Professor of Law at the Louisiana State University Law Center and director of the program in Law, Science, and Public Health.

Public health authorities have all the emergency powers they need to enforce quarantines and protect the public—more laws are unnecessary. However, public health officials and institutions do need more money to hire workers and staff. They also need government support for policies, such as paid sick leave for workers, which could reduce the spread of infectious diseases. Unfortunately, politicians prefer to pass dramatic emergency powers rather than make real, costly investments in public health.

As this is being written [May 2009], H1N1 is not a major threat, but this could change as the epidemic evolves. I want to look past the H1N1 outbreak and focus attention on what we will carry away from it, however it evolves. I am concerned because crisis-driven policy is easy to hijack, resulting in laws with horrible unintended consequences. Over the past four decades, public health crises have generated more than their share of bad laws. Some only create false expectations, but others have led to great suffering and even death. I hope forewarned is forearmed for H1N1.

Ed Richards, "Fighting H1N1: Why Laws Are Not the Answer," *Jurist*, May 2, 2009. Copyright © Bernard J. Hibbitts 2009. Reproduced by permission of the author.

Do We Need More Law?

It is not law *per se* that I worry about. I am quite supportive of public health law as expressed through administrative regulations and the broad exercise of the police powers. [Although] public health depends primarily on voluntary cooperation, state public health agencies and the federal government have tremendous powers to deal with a public health crisis. The United States entered the 1970s with a public health system that had nearly tripled life expectancy over the [previous] 100 years through sanitation, which had nearly wiped out the worst of the communicable diseases in the [United States], and which was immunizing a sizable part of the population against seasonal flu. All this, including the quarantine of individuals and whole regions, had been managed through general grants of legislative power and administrative regulations. This framework has not been declared unconstitutional, and as classic administrative law, there is no reason to think the U.S. Supreme Court would stop deferring to agency action in public health when it supports agency deference in all other areas of administrative law.

Many states still have laws in place that limit disease control efforts for HIV.

What I worry about are statutes, i.e., specific public health policies passed into statutes to please interest groups. From quarantining people who are coughing to taxing fat people, pushing for public health statutes has become the rage at the CDC [Centers for Disease Control and Prevention], federal and state legislatures, and private foundations. These are driven by traditional interest groups, such as employers worried about health care costs, drug companies, military contractors who want to sell bioterrorism monitors, and federal officials in recent administrations who wanted to extend the national security state.

The last decade has seen a new interest group arise: contract researchers, operating out of universities, who live on grant funds to write new laws. No matter the problem, their solution is a new law, because they make no money if they admit that the problem is just that public health agencies do not have the staff to do a job because they are broke, or that there is no problem at all. Expect to see these groups calling for massive new public health powers to deal with H1N1, claiming that public health agencies and the federal government lack key powers. As noted below, public health emergencies are fully integrated into our national security laws, allowing the federal government essentially unlimited powers if it chooses to use them. Perhaps the only real limit is that since President Obama repudiated the torture memos, the torture of potential disease carriers is now off limits.

We have created a system ... whose real purpose is to allow legislatures to claim to have done something about public health emergencies without spending the money or political capital to address the weakness in the public health and medical care system.

Unintended Consequences

Concerns with the public health consequences of illegal drug use in the 1960s led to Nixon's war on drugs and Rockefeller's draconian drug laws, which spread across the United States. These laws have had profound unintended consequences and seem to slip the mind of public health law scholars who tout the value of new public health statutes. In the 1980s, civil libertarians lobbied state legislatures and Congress to protect persons with AIDS. The result was to make it nearly impossible to do public health screening and case finding for HIV infection. This exacerbated the AIDS epidemic and was only reversed as a matter of federal policy in 2006. Many states still have laws in place that limit disease control efforts for HIV. (In several states, the entire disease control code was revised, undermining the control of tuberculosis and other diseases. These laws had to be revised again as tuberculosis surged in the 1990s.)

Post 9/11 and the anthrax letters [when letters containing antrax were sent to government officials and media outlets in 2001], fears of bioterrorism led the CDC to develop the Model State Emergency Health Powers Act and push states to adopt it. This was criticized by many public law scholars for being a dangerous intrusion into civil liberties and probably also unworkable. More fundamentally, if you are versed in national security law, you know that the push for public health emergency powers laws at the state and federal level were derived from the [President George W. Bush/Vice President Dick Cheney] vision of the seamless national security state. Taken with the Patriot Act and other national security laws [enacted after the 9/11 attacks to expand government powers in terrorism investigations], public health and safety emergencies have been recharacterized as national security threats, which creates paths for the use of the military in domestic policing and the overruling of state public health authority by the federal government.

The real problem with all of these laws is that the problems they address are not problems of legal authority. They do nothing to address the loss of resources and expertise from health departments, [or] the weakness of political leaders when facing difficult choices. We have created a system of Potemkin laws [impressive in appearance only; sham] whose real purpose is to allow legislatures to claim to have done something about public health emergencies without spending the money or political capital to address the weakness in the public health and medical care system. Look how well these laws worked [after] Hurricane Katrina [which struck Louisiana in 2005]. Louisiana had passed stacks of emergency powers laws after 9/11, had done all the federal planning exercises, yet was completely unprepared for Hurricane Katrina, because that would have required spending money and admitting that New Orleans could flood. Yet Katrina spawned another deluge of federal and state emergency powers laws, passed as states continued to cut their already inadequate health department budgets.

SARS and H1N1

The most recent failure, and the one most on point with H1N1, was the reaction to the 2003 SARS [a respiratory illness which killed hundreds in China and worldwide] outbreak. Canada appointed a royal commission to study and make recommendations about the lessons learned from SARS. The commission published an excellent set of reports on all aspects of the SARS epidemic and the government's response. The commission was clear: strategies such as social distancing, not going to work sick, and voluntary isolation can work only if the affected individuals are supported by the employers and the government. Individuals must have paid sick leave, worker's compensation must cover workplace-acquired infection, there must be health insurance coverage for personally acquired illness, and employers and others institutions must work out the details of mandatory immunization programs with unions and workers before there is an outbreak.

The Canadians found little or no role for coercion, but a critical role for the government and employers to provide support to allow individuals to stay home without loss of income and with adequate medical care and food. The response in the United States was to pass even more quarantine laws, to provide bench books to judges on how to enforce those laws, and to encourage local law enforcement to think about their rules of engagement when enforcing quarantine—do you shoot the soccer mom fleeing with the minivan full of children?

There have been no provisions for the nearly half of workers without paid sick leave, for workers with infected family members who will lose pay if they stay home, for health care for the uninsured. The huge population of undocumented aliens and the legal and illegal underground economy have been ignored, yet we know those who participate in the underground economy are not likely to honor snow days and other social distancing strategies because they do not eat if they do not work.

The best outcome for H1N1 is that we have relatively few cases and deaths, we will develop a vaccine over the summer [2009], we will conduct an orderly vaccination program in the fall, and H1N1 will become just one virus on the list we consider for each seasonal flu vaccine. (For perspective, remember that yearly flu outbreak results in a few million cases and 10,000–20,000 deaths, with no great disruption in life and the economy.) We will look back and realize that it would have been nice to have more epidemiologists in the states [that experienced] cases, and the states and the federal government will increase funding and job protections for expert staff at health departments.

More likely, whatever the outcome of H1N1, the result will be more laws benefiting more interest groups and politicians' reelection campaigns, and no long-term support for the public health system.

Organizations to Contact

The editors have compiled the following list of organizations concerned with the issues debated in this book. The descriptions are derived from materials provided by the organizations. All have publications or information available for interested readers. The list was compiled on the date of publication of the present volume; names, addresses, phone and fax numbers, and e-mail and Internet addresses may change. Be aware that many organizations take several weeks or longer to respond to inquiries, so allow as much time as possible.

American Red Cross
2025 E Street NW, Washington, DC   20006
(202) 303-4498
Web site: www.redcross.org

The American Red Cross is a humanitarian agency that provides aid for those affected by natural and other disasters. Since the initial H1N1 outbreak in April, the American Red Cross has been helping individuals, families, schools, businesses and organizations prepare for and take action to reduce the spread of H1N1 influenza in their communities. Red Cross also continues to monitor the situation in coordination with federal and state officials. The Red Cross's Web site includes news updates and fact sheets on the virus, including the leaflet "Preparing for a H1N1 (Swine Flu) Pandemic."

Centers for Disease Control and Prevention (CDC)
1600 Clifton Road, Atlanta, GA   30333
(404) 639-3534
Web site: www.cdc.gov

The CDC, founded in 1946, was originally charged with the task of finding methods to control malaria. Since its inception, the organization's mission has broadened, but there is still a focus on preventing and managing both communicable and noncommunicable diseases. The CDC offers guidelines for professionals and the general public on how to behave in order to slow or prevent the spread of infectious disease. The organization also provides extensive research on the ways in which vaccinations are administered, the possibility of future pandemics, and new methods to prevent pandemics. Two topical publications by the CDC are *Emerging Infectious Diseases Journal* and *Preventing Chronic Disease Journal*.

Childhood Influenza Immunization Coalition (CIIC)

90 Fifth Ave., Suite 800, New York, NY   10011-2052
(212) 886-2277
E-mail: CIIC@nfid.org
Web site: www.preventchildhoodinfluenza.org

The CIIC was established by the National Foundation for Infectious Diseases (NFID) to protect infants, children, and adolescents from influenza by communicating the need to make influenza immunization a national health priority and by seeking to improve the low influenza immunization rates among children. Its members represent twenty-five of the nation's leading public health, medical, patient and parent groups. Its Web site includes information for the media, health care professionals, and the public, including the report *Improving Childhood Influenza Immunization Rates to Protect Our Nation's Children*.

Children's Hospital of Philadelphia Vaccine Education Center

The Children's Hospital of Philadelphia
Philadelphia, PA   19104
(215) 590-100
Web site: www.vaccine.chop.edu

The Children's Hospital of Philadelphia is one of the leading pediatric hospitals and research facilities in the world. Its vaccine Web site contains detailed information about each available vaccine, plus the answers to general questions about vaccination. The site includes a link to the downloadable factsheet "Novel H1N1 and the Vaccine," and instructions on how to receive the "Parents Pack Monthly Newsletter," which deals with vaccination issues.

Department of Health and Human Services (HHS)
200 Independence Ave. SW, Washington, DC   20201
(202) 691-0257
Web site: www.hhs.gov

The HHS is the U.S. government agency that concentrates on the public's health and well-being. It is the parent agency of other government health organizations such as the CDC and the National Institutes of Health. Among the agency's many services, disease prevention and immunization are top priorities. The HHS manages many services dedicated not only to researching new options to combat disease but also to create informative programs for the public. The Web site includes numerous documents relating to H1N1, including factsheets, news reports, transcripts of Senate testimony, and other materials.

Infectious Diseases Society of America (IDSA)
66 Canal Center Plaza, Suite 600, Alexandria, VA   22314
(703) 299-0200 • fax (702) 299-0204
E-mail: info@idsociety.org
Web site: www.idsociety.org

The IDSA is an organization of health care and scientific professionals concerned with the prevention and treatment of infectious diseases. The society provides research suggesting how to provide the best care for individuals with communicable diseases. The IDSA also works as an advocacy group promoting sound public policy on infectious diseases. IDSA's Web site includes many resources focused on H1N1, including "Influenza H1N1: Frontline Questions and Expert Opinion Answers," a collaborative fact page written by leading flu experts. In addition to the *IDSA News*, the society publishes the journals *Clinical Infectious Diseases* and the *Journal of Infectious Diseases*.

National Network for Immunization Information (NNII)

301 University Blvd., Galveston, TX   77555-0351
(409) 772-01991 • Fax: (409) 747-4995
E-mail: nnii@i4ph.org
Web site: www.immunizationinfo.org

The aim of the NNII is to provide the public, health professionals, policy makers, and the media with up-to-date, scientifically valid information related to immunization in order to help them understand the issues and to make informed decisions. Its Web site has fact sheets and information about flu and flu vaccines.

National Vaccine Information Center (NVIC)

204 Mill Street, Suite B1, Vienna, VA   22180
(703) 938-0342 • Fax: (703) 938-5768
Web site: www.nvic.org

The NVIC, a national, nonprofit educational organization, is the oldest and largest consumer organization advocating the institution of vaccine safety and informed consent protections in the mass vaccination system. It is dedicated to the prevention of vaccine injuries and deaths through public education. As an independent clearinghouse for information on diseases and vaccines, NVIC does not promote the use of vaccines and does not advise against the use of vaccines; it supports the availability of all preventive health care options and the right of consumers to make educated, voluntary health care choices. NVIC publshes a free newsletter, and its Web site includes fact sheets and articles, including "H1N1: Fact or Fiction," and "Swine Flu Vaccine: Will We Have a Choice?"

United States Agency for International Development (USAID)

Information Center, Ronald Reagan Building
Washington, DC   20523-1000
(202) 712-4810 • fax (202) 216-3524
Web site: www.usaid.gov

USAID is an international aid organization of the U.S. government. Program goals include disaster relief, aid for countries attempting to end poverty, and promotion of democratic reform. One important facet addressed in order to achieve these goals is disease prevention and management. USAID provides programs and funding to aid in the fight against these pandemics worldwide. USAID's monthly news publication, *Frontlines*, is published in print and electronically. The site also includes numerous press releases and fact sheets relating to H1N1.

World Health Organization (WHO)
525 23rd Street NW, Washington, DC   20037
(202) 974-3000 • fax (202) 974-3663
E-mail: postmaster@paho.org
Web site: www.who.int

The WHO is a United Nations agency formed in 1948 with the goal of creating and ensuring a world where all people can live with high levels of both mental and physical health. The organization researches and endorses different methods of combating the spread of diseases such as malaria, SARS, and H1N1. The WHO publishes the *Bulletin of the World Health Organization*, which is available online, as well as the *Pan American Journal of Public Health*. Within the WHO, the Pan American Health Organization is the regional office that covers the United States.

Bibliography

Books

Thomas Abraham *Twenty-First Century Plague: The Story of SARS.* Baltimore, MD: Johns Hopkins University Press, 2005.

Philip Alcabes *Dread: How Fear and Fantasy Have Fueled Epidemics from the Black Death to the Avian Flu.* New York, NY: Perseus Books, 2009.

Arthur Allen *Vaccine: The Controversial Story of Medicine's Greatest Lifesaver.* New York, NY: W.W. Norton & Company, 2007.

Jennifer Brower *The Global Threat of New and Reemerging Infectious Disease: Reconciling U.S. National Security and Public Health Policy.* Santa Monica, CA: Rand, 2003.

John M. Dorrance *Global Time Bomb: Surviving the H1N1 Swine Flue Pandemic and Other Global Health Threats.* Vancouver Island, Canada: Madrona Books, 2009.

Laurie Garrett *Betrayal of Trust: The Collapse of Global Public Health.* New York, NY: Hyperion, 2000.

Laurie Garrett   *The Coming Plague: Newly Emerging Diseases in a World Out of Balance.* New York, NY: Penguin Books, 1994.

Denise Grady   *Deadly Invaders: Virus Outbreaks Around the World, from Marburg Fever to Avian Flu.* Boston, MA: Kingfisher, 2006.

Karl Taro Greenfeld   *China Syndrome: The True Story of the 21st Century's First Great Epidemic.* New York, NY: HarperCollins, 2006

Michael Greger   *Bird Flu: A Virus of Our Own Hatching.* New York, NY: Lantern Books, 2006.

Karen Peebles   *2009 Swine Flu Outbreak.* Createspace, 2009.

Dorothy A. Pettit   *A Cruel Mind: Pandemic Flu in America 1918–1920.* Murfreesboro, TN: Timberland Books, 2008.

Tom Quinn   *Flu: A Social History of Influenza.* London, UK: New Holland Publishers, 2008.

Robert Sears   *The Vaccine Book: Making the Right Decision for Your Child.* New York, NY: Little, Brown, 2007.

Viroj Wiwanitkit   *Swine Flu and Pig Borne Diseases.* Hauppage, NY: Nova Science Publishers, Inc., 2009.

Periodicals

Jackie Calmes and Donald G. McNeil, Jr.	"H1N1 Is Still Spreading Globally," *New York Times*, October 25, 2009.
Centers For Disease Prevention and Control	"2009 H1N1 Flu ('Swine Flu') and You," January 12, 2010. www.cdc.gov.
CNN.com	"Obama Declares H1N1 Emergency," October 26, 2009.
Ariana Eunjung Cha	"Caught in China's Aggressive Swine Flu Net," *Washington Post*, May 29, 2009.
Economist	"Down with the Flu," October 16, 2009.
Megan Fitzpatrick	"Brace for More H1N1 Deaths, Canada's Top Doctor Warns," *Vancouver Sun*, November 5, 2006.
V. Dion Haynes and Ylan Q. Mui	"H1N1 Exposes Weak Leave Policies," *Washington Post*, November 9, 2009.
Lucy Hornby	"China Credits Quarantine for Containing H1N1," Reuters.com, June 11, 2009.
Hilary Kramer	"Don't Underestimate the Impact of H1N1," *Huffington Post*, January 4, 2010.

Andrew Malcolm	"Dr. Ron Paul Calls Obama's H1N1 Swine Flu Program a 'Total Failure,'" *Top of the Ticket*, October 31, 2009. http://latimesblogs.latimes.com.
Maggie Mertens	"Sick-Leave Legislation Gets a Boost from H1N1," *Shots*, November 11, 2009. www.npr.org.
MSNBC	"Mexico Flu Deaths Raise Fears of Global Epidemic," April 24, 2009.
Alice Park and Bryan Walsh	"Early Data Show H1N1 Vaccine Is Highly Effective," *Time*, September 10, 2009.
Robert Schlesinger	"Whether to Get the H1N1 Vaccine," usnews.com, October 15, 2009.
Marc Siegel	"Blowing the Shot," *Slate*, November 2, 2009. www.slate.com.
Jake Tapper	"Obama Administration: Out With the 'Swine,' in With the 'H1N1 Virus,'" *Political Punch*, April 29, 2009. http://blogs.abcnews.com.
Bryan Walsh	"Was the Alarm over Swine Flu Justified?" *Time*, May 4, 2009.
Kevin Whitelaw	"Flu, Me? Public Remains Wary of H1N1 Vaccine," NPR Online, October 17, 2009.

Index